RADICAL POLITICS IN MODERN IRELAND

This photograph of 15 members of the ISRP appeared in *The Irish Times* on the fortieth anniversary of the execution of James Connolly (courtesy of *The Irish Times* and probably given by William O'Brien).

Radical Politics in Modern Ireland

The Irish Socialist Republican Party
1896–1904

DAVID LYNCH

IRISH ACADEMIC PRESS
DUBLIN • PORTLAND, OR

First published in 2005 by
IRISH ACADEMIC PRESS
44, Northumberland Road, Dublin 4, Ireland
and in the United States of America by
IRISH ACADEMIC PRESS
c/o ISBS, Suite 300
920 NE 58th Avenue
Portland, Oregon 97213-3644

Website: www.iap.ie

© David Lynch 2005

British Library Cataloguing in Publication Data

A catalogue entry is available by request

ISBN 0-7 165-3356-1 (cloth)

Library of Congress Cataloging-in-Publication Data

A catalog entry is available by request

Typeset in 10.5/13pt Palatino by FiSH Books, London
Printed by MPG Books Limited, Bodmin, Cornwall

Contents

Acknowledgements

Firstly, I would like to thank everyone at Irish Academic Press for showing faith in the project. In particular I want to thank my editor Lisa Hyde and the anonymous reader of the early draft. I would like to mention the staff of the National Library of Ireland (NLI), where I have spent many hours in recent years. I want to also thank all my friends and family for their support during a period where it must have seemed like I was talking about the ISRP and James Connolly for ever. In particular a special word for my parents David and Marie Lynch for their continued unconditionally support in everything I have done, including this project. This support included the not-so insignificant gift of allowing me complete access to their 'computer facilities' while writing this book. In this regard I also want to mention my sister Julie Lynch who provided constant 'technical support' when I had problems with the computer and printer. My friends Mark Walsh and Simon Dunne also deserve special mention for their years of friendship and intellectual comradeship since college and beyond. In early 2004 my friend Stephen Griffin tragically died far away from home. The fun and friendship he brought into many of our lives is greatly missed. This book is dedicated to his memory. Finally, I want to thank my fellow NUI Maynooth graduate Anne Marie Quinn. Her bright and questioning mind was a great help in the early drafts of the book. But her help extended far beyond this with her constant encouragement, meaning that I finally got around to stop talking about James Connolly and the ISRP and started the more laborious (but eventually more rewarding) task of writing about them.

In memory of Stephen Griffin (1978–2004)

Abbreviations

CPI	Communist Party of Ireland
GAA	Gaelic Athletic Association
ICA	Irish Citizen Army
ILP	Independent Labour Party
ILP(I)	Independent Labour Party of Ireland
IRB	Irish Republican Brotherhood
ITUC	Irish Trades Union Congress
ITGWU	Irish Transport and General Workers Union
ISRP	Irish Socialist Republican Party
LEA	Labour Electoral Association (Ireland)
NLI	National Library of Ireland
SDF	Social Democratic Federation (Great Britain)
SPA	Socialist Party of America
SPD	*Sozialdemokratische Partei Deutschlands* (Social Democratic Party of Germany)
SPI	Socialist Party of Ireland
SLP	Socialist Labour Party (Ireland)
SLP	Socialist Labour Party (United States)
SSF	Scottish Socialist Federation
UIL	United Irish League

Foreword

This illuminating and insightful book is dominated by characters that were imbued with vigour, intellect and a commitment to an improvement in the lives of working class people. It captures the ethos of a party that, if mentioned by historians in the past, has merited only a passing reference. This is not a partisan account, but a balanced probing of the rise and fall of the ISRP, and the result has filled a major gap in our knowledge and understanding of Irish labour history in the late nineteenth and early twentieth century.

Lynch does not exaggerate the influence or membership of the ISRP, but he does effectively chart the determination of a number of individuals to employ the word 'Republic' and 'Socialist' in the same context, and who refused to await the endorsement of middle-class Ireland. The appearance of Ireland's first regular socialist newspaper – the *Workers' Republic* – was one of their notable achievements. James Connolly is a towering presence, but the author has also done justice to many other characters – Dan O'Brien, Con O'Lyhane, Edward Stewart and Fred Ryan among others; young and bohemian characters who added colour and passion to Dublin and Cork over one hundred years ago.

At one of the earlier ISRP meetings, one of the questions discussed was 'Are we Utopians?'. Perhaps they were, but what is striking is how enduring and far-sighted the party's programme was, and how relevant the issues they raised still remain, including free education, free maintenance for children, legislative restrictions on the hours of labour, a minimum wage and the modernisation of agriculture. They also made the connection between imperialism, capitalism and war before many other socialists. Their political vision was also concerned with Irish socialism in an international context, and when attending the International Socialist Congress in Paris in 1900, they insisted, successfully, on being accepted as Irish representatives, and not as a mere section of the British delegation.

Not surprisingly, rhetoric abounded, but putting their socialist theory into practice was a sobering experience. To the author's credit, he does not romanticise or sentimentalise the party or its programme. It faced huge difficulties, including church hostility, and never had an active membership of more than 80.

But the enormous workload of particular activists reflected a determination to fight against the odds. The tensions within the labour movement are highlighted; in particular the reluctance to endorse strikes and the hostility that existed between the ISRP and the Labour Electoral Association.

Lynch also acknowledges the weaknesses of the party both organisationally and in terms of personality. Connolly maintained, with a measure of truth, that the votes they received 'were cast for socialism in spite of a campaign of calumny unequalled in its infamy'. But there was also a tendency to continually blame their opponents at the expense of self-critical analysis, an over reliance on propaganda, a naïve belief that Republicans would eventually be won over to a socialist philosophy, and a neglect of the Protestant Loyalist working class. Connolly's censorship of any discussion of religion was counterproductive and unreasonable. Nor does the author shy away from revising accepted historical wisdom – he challenges, for example, the notion that they were instinctively hostile to the cultural revival.

Drink, bullying, personal abuse, financial rows and expulsion all played a part in the party's demise. But ultimately, it was ideological differences, by no means confined to Ireland, which hampered them, particularly the debate as to whether socialism could be progressed through reform or revolution. This book admirably highlights the sacrifices that they all made, personally and financially, in order to try and achieve, as Robert Lynd put it, 'a richer individual life both for human beings and for nations'. It may be true, as the author contends, that the ISRP created a radical space and then squandered it; but that they created such a space at all, given the formidable obstacles, was a significant achievement. David Lynch has told their story lucidly, originally and fairly, and in the process has rectified an unjustifiable neglect of some of the pioneers of modern Irish socialism.

Diarmaid Ferriter
February 2005

Introduction

Our army marches onward with its face towards the dawn,
In trust secure in that one thing the slave may lean upon;
The might within the arm of him who, knowing Freedom's worth,
Strikes home to banish tyranny from off the face of Earth.
                                        – James Connolly, *A Rebel Song*[1]

A picture taken of fifteen members of the Irish Socialist Republican Party (ISRP) in May 1901 shows men, many of whose names are long forgotten in the history of the Irish labour movement. These men were the pioneers of modern socialist and republican politics in Ireland. Some of them – William O'Brien, Edward Stewart and, of course, James Connolly – have etched out a place for themselves in Irish labour history. However, the majority of those young faces staring at the camera have found themselves consigned, to what the Russian revolutionary Leon Trotsky described as the 'dustbin of history'.[2] This study is an attempt to place the ISRP in its proper historical context and to show in detail how the organisation, notwithstanding its paltry official membership, represents a profound moment in the development of socialism and republicanism in Ireland's political history.

The ISRP was Ireland's first socialist republican party and thus was the founding father (for all the members were men) of the modern socialist and republican movement in Ireland. While there had been small socialist and sometimes larger advanced nationalist groupings active in Ireland before the formation of the ISRP in 1896, the major ideological and practical break that the ISRP represented was recognised both by contemporaries of the period and by those working in the Irish labour movement in the decades following the demise of the ISRP in 1904. The ISRP was the forerunner and ideological springhead for an important political tradition that has had a significant impact on radical Irish politics ever since.

In the period between the death of the Home Rule Party 'Chief' Charles Stewart Parnell in 1891 and the Proclamation of the Irish Republic on the steps of the GPO in April 1916, Ireland witnessed a blazing battle between many competing ideologies, from a range of political, social and cultural sources. These ideologies were attempting to win the adherence of the Irish people, and to shape the social and political future of the island. The fluid and transitory nature of this period often leaves the historian dizzy when it is compared to the predictability (on the surface at least) of life under the Chief's leadership of the Irish Home Rule Party. Yet with Parnell's personal and political collapse following the famous divorce trial involving Katherine O'Shea, and the resulting split in the Home Rule Party, a vacuum was created that sucked into it all manner of competing political discourses, discourses that eventually decided the political framework of the new Irish nation.[3]

The future leader of Fianna Fàil and Irish Taoiseach Eamon de Valera's famous advice to the left wing of the struggle for national independence was 'labour must wait' – meaning that those who wanted to establish socialism in Ireland should keep their political powder dry until the 'national question' had been resolved. As many acquainted with the history of Irish left-wing politics know, Irish labour dutifully acquiesced to de Valera's request and stood no candidates in the momentous elections of 1918. Yet that famous assertion has a much deeper resonance within the history of left-wing politics than that of the elections of 1918. Irish history, as it was written in the early decades of the Irish Free State, was very much a story of Irish labour waiting around while the great debates regarding the 'land issue', 'religious identity' and, of course, the ubiquitous 'national question' were played out with little or no involvement by the political adherents of socialism in Ireland. This lack of labour analysis within historiography was a product of the weakness of the left-wing political tradition in Ireland following 'independence'. Ireland has not seen the growth of any sizeable socialist movement over the past eighty years, unlike the majority of other European nations. This simple observation by F.S.L. Lyons in his *Ireland Since the Famine*, first published in 1963, remains a point of constant interest to the historian of modern Irish history:

No one who casts even the most cursory glance over modern Irish history can fail to be struck either by the slowness with which anything remotely recognisable as a labour movement emerged, or by the relative feebleness of that movement when it did emerge.[4]

The lack of influence of the labour movement in the Irish state following the War of Independence led to an almost complete ignorance regarding labour politics before 1922 in Irish historiography. This is most clearly the case with the political legacy of James Connolly. In the early decades of the new Irish state the socialist left-wing component of Connolly's philosophy and politics was deliberately downplayed, while an image of Connolly as a 'nationalist martyr' was actively promoted by the new conservative Irish establishment. As the story goes, it is principally the victors who write history, and by any set of standards Irish labour was far from victorious after the foundation of the Irish Free State. Yet recent studies of socialism in Ireland before 1896, the momentous events of the Great Lock-Out of 1913, the Limerick 'Soviet' of 1919 and the active role played by the Irish working class in the War of Independence among other topics, have shed new light on the history of labour in the important years before the signing of the Anglo-Irish Treaty in late 1921.[5]

In the years between the fall of Parnell and the Easter Rising Ireland went through a process of rapid invention. The twenty-six county Free State's eventual identity as principally confessional, conservative, Gaelic in aspiration, rural and indeed capitalist was created during this period. However, just because this was the outcome does not mean that it had to be so. The future of Ireland was 'up for grabs' during that period, as the social and political milieu became diverse and heterogeneous following the split in the Home Rule Party, a profound political event that ended that organisation's hegemonic hold over the Irish people's political allegiances.

In the vacuum created by the split in the Home Rule Party all manner of political, cultural, literary, sporting and identity politics rushed in to try to help to forge the bond that was needed to build an 'imagined community' from which the new Irish state was to find its identity.[6] The Gaelic League, the Irish Literary Revival, the Gaelic Athletic Association (GAA), the United Irish League (UIL) and Sinn Féin, all swirled around the melting pot that was Ireland at the turn of the nineteenth and twentieth centuries.

Labour politics played an important role in this period and for a time the ISRP was the principal organisation engaged in raising the level of consciousness in the country regarding socialist politics. Of course labour politics failed to win the adherence of enough workers in Ireland to influence to any significant extent the shape of the Irish political scene after 1922. Class identity eventually came a poor third after religious and national identity among the island's population, but this was not a predetermined or constant situation.

The ISRP, founded by James Connolly and a small number of fellow socialists in 1896, was an expression of labour, for once, refusing to wait for the approval of 'nationalist Ireland' before making a political push for socialism. The ISRP proclaimed itself in favour of a 'Workers' Republic' at least a decade before the term 'republic' became commonplace in the vernacular of political Ireland. As an organisation it straddled the two centuries, collapsing in 1904 after eight years as the primary force agitating in favour of socialism in Ireland.

During its short period in existence the actual achievements of the ISRP were impressive for such a small organisation. The party produced the first regular socialist paper in Ireland, the *Workers' Republic*; it ran candidates in local elections; it represented Ireland in the Second International, a major force on the European political landscape at the time; it agitated over issues such as the Boer War and the 1798 centenary commemorations gaining much notoriety among the Irish press and public by its behaviour; it produced copious amounts of written propaganda and held open public meetings; and it attempted to establish branches in Cork and Belfast, beyond its base in Dublin.

However, the lasting influence of the party did not principally stem from its activity between 1896 and 1904. Rather, the programme and political outlook of the party represent a fundamental break from what had existed before within the Irish 'advanced nationalist' and socialist groupings. Further, the ISRP was one of the first socialist groups working within a colonised nation to agitate for socialism and to take a political stand against imperialism.

The arrival of James Connolly in Dublin in 1896 and the formation of the ISRP in the same year represent a watershed in Irish labour politics. The party was Marxist, internationalist, and linked, theoretically and practically, with the international socialist movement, and it attempted to use the theory of 'scientific socialism' to explain the social ills suffered by the Irish working class of the period. The party also united the call for an independent Ireland with the call for workers' control of industry and agriculture within a socialist Ireland. Rather than ignoring or downplaying the nationalist question, something so many socialists had done before and have done since, the party tackled the issue of Ireland's self-determination head on, and declared that the struggle for a nation independent from the British Empire and the struggle for a socialist Ireland were not competing aspirations, but complementary.

The significance of the ISRP in the history of modern Irish republicanism lies in its role as the first organised expression of the leftist and socially concerned side of the republican movement. While the political genealogy of much of modern republicanism is traced back to the formation of Arthur Griffith's Sinn Féin party in 1908, many who have considered themselves 'republican' over the past one hundred years would have had more in common with the economic and political theories of Connolly and the ISRP than with the capitalist, protectionist model espoused by Griffith. The ISRP was the first experiment with that powerful, dynamic, yet sometimes very confused cocktail of traditional republican politics and socialist principles.

The ISRP has never received the political and historical attention that it deserves considering the impact the organisation has had on the radical tradition in Ireland. The party itself has not been the subject of any major historical analysis, with the partial exception of Sean Cronin's informative short study of Connolly's early political life in Ireland, *Young Connolly*.[7] In Peter Berresford Ellis's otherwise fairly definitive *A History of the Irish Working Class* the party receives attention over just three pages out of 370.[8] This apparent oversight is understandable, however. The membership of the ISRP was always small in number. The jibe that it had 'more initials than members'[9] was not just a bit of banter from political enemies, but a statement that carried much truth. Some historians have seen the party as being little more than an ideological vehicle for its founder and leading member, James Connolly. Thus Emmet O'Connor wrote that the 'energy, policies, and significance' of the ISRP 'derived entirely' from Connolly.[10]

However, other historians have argued for the seminal importance that the foundation of the ISRP has in the history of Irish socialism and republicanism. Fintan Lane, who has done much to uncover the origins of modern Irish socialism before the arrival of Connolly in 1896, still concludes that it is difficult to overestimate 'the enormity of the redirection prompted by the political thought of Connolly and the Irish Socialist Republican Party (ISRP). After 1896 a version of Marxism emerged that has remained potently influential on the Irish left ever since.'[11] Connolly was undoubtedly the leading intellectual power in the party and the powerful bedrock on which the edifice of the party was built. Thus the ISRP has normally provided a chapter or two in the numerous political biographies that have been written about the ISRP's founder and the eventual martyr of the 1916 Rising.

Whatever about the historians, there can be little doubt regarding how important the early participants in the history of Irish labour believed the ISRP to be. Connolly himself described the collapse and demise of the organisation as 'like losing a child', and the failure of the organisation to grow remained one of his chief political regrets. In 1919, at the Berne Conference of the Socialist International, the future leader of the Irish Labour Party, Thomas Johnson, made it quite clear in an address on the state of the Irish political left that the ISRP was the seed from which the Irish labour movement had grown: 'Connolly and the Irish Socialist Republican Party were the pioneers of proletarian Socialism in Ireland, and the first to give the Irish workers a definite and class conscious Socialist organisation.'[12]   Johnson made this address on behalf of the Socialist Party of Ireland (SPI), the Irish Labour Party and the Irish trade union movement. All the major groupings on the political left from 1916 through the period of the War of Independence claimed at least some of their heritage from the ISRP. The party had a direct organisational link with the far left that emerged in Ireland after Independence, in the form of the various Communist splinter groups; it also had a link, both organisationally and in terms of personnel, with the Labour Party, founded in 1912, and it had a significant influence on the political philosophy of the left of the republican movement from 1904 onwards.

Writing from his prolific pen in the United States in 1909, five years after the demise of the party, Connolly made it clear how much of a watershed he himself believed the formation of the party to have been and emphasised the importance of the theoretical stance it took in favour of creating a Workers' Republic in Ireland:

> It is no exaggeration to say that this organisation and its policy completely revolutionised advanced politics in Ireland. When it was first initiated the word 'republic' was looked upon as a word to be only whispered among intimates; the Socialists boldly advised the driving from public life of all those who would not openly accept it. The thought of revolution was the exclusive possession of a few remnants of the secret societies of a past generation, and was never mentioned by them except with heads closely together and eyes fearfully glancing around; the Socialists broke through this

ridiculous secrecy, and in hundreds of speeches in the most public places of the metropolis, as well as in scores of thousands of pieces of literature scattered through the country, announced their purpose to muster all the forces of labour for a revolutionary reconstruction of society and the incidental destruction of the British Empire.[13]

The lasting influence of the party on the radical political left in Ireland cannot be overestimated. The party combined a heady mixture of socialism and republicanism that continues to have a major bearing on the politics of today. The attempts by the ISRP to deal with the 'national question' through the political prism of socialism began a debate that was to occupy the minds of many within the radical political tradition in Ireland throughout the twentieth century.

This study will attempt to redress the lack of historical investigation into the party and place the ISRP in its proper context, both ideologically and through its actions in this important period of flux in Irish political history.

A history of this nature has a number of major difficulties inherent within it, not least, as has been highlighted earlier, the fact that this numerically small organisation was dominated by one major figure. James Connolly was the 'presiding genius of the whole business', the most active member and the leading theoretical light in the party.[14] He was the unofficial leader of the organisation and the editor of the ISRP's paper. Hence it is difficult to give voice to the other members of the party through the primary sources available to us. Where it has been possible to write of the ISRP rather than just Connolly we have tried to do so, although in many ways the stories of both Connolly and the ISRP overlap one another. Yet it must be said that Connolly, notwithstanding his undoubted political brilliance, could not have built up the organisation without the help of his comrades: the party was more than just one man and Connolly himself recognised this fact.

Chapter One describes the Ireland in which Connolly and the ISRP attempted to sow the seeds of socialism. Home Rule and the Land War dominated the political agenda of the time, and the full significance of the fall of Parnell and the split in the Home Rule Party had yet to be made clear. The Irish working class was numerically small and clustered into a tiny number of urban areas. Yet, despite this, the first steps towards the creation of trade unions were taken.

This chapter also investigates the formation of the party and its internal workings in the first years of its existence. It takes a detailed look at the radical programme of the ISRP, and views it in both its Irish context and its international context. The involvement of the ISRP in the 1798 centenary commemorations and the protests against the Jubilee celebrations in 1897 are also investigated. The ISRP called for the political independence of Ireland for very different reasons from those of Karl Marx and the other founders of the socialist movement: this chapter teases out these differences. By focusing on what the early socialists wrote about Ireland, this chapter emphasises the theoretical break that the ISRP made from the earlier socialist tradition on the issue of Ireland's self-determination.

Chapter Two discusses the importance of the publication of the *Workers' Republic*. Ireland's first Marxist newspaper was to be the ideological mouthpiece for the party and Connolly in particular. The relationship between the ISRP and the wider labour movement, including the Labour Electoral Association (LEA) and the trade unions is also discussed. The party took a strong anti-imperialist line and the Boer War gave the ISRP an opportunity to express that in a very practical way. We look into the source of this 'anti-imperialism' and chart the nature of the protests organised on the streets of Dublin by the party against the Boer conflict.

In Chapter Three we turn our attention to the electoral work engaged in by the ISRP, which began with the local elections of January 1899. The ISRP is again viewed within its international context, as part of the Second International, as well as through its links with the British labour movement, which became strained over time.

Although small in size and influence, the ISRP participated in the great political debates of the day. Chapter Four deals with the political stance of the ISRP on three of the major issues occupying the minds of Irish people during the period: land, religion and nationalism.

Chapter Five chronicles the bitter demise of the party in the early months of 1903 and into 1904. While this is viewed in most historical accounts as a petty squabble among party members, this study proposes that the split in the party reflected a much larger and more fundamental schism then developing within the international socialist movement, between those in favour of reforming capitalism as an end in itself and those socialists who still believed in following the more revolutionary road to overthrowing the economic system.

Chapter Six describes how the influence of the party has echoed down the subsequent history of the Irish labour movement, charting the legacy of the ISRP from the momentous period of the War of Independence through the history of the Irish state until the present day.

While the party was a 'failure' in one sense of the word, the ISRP did contribute a radical leftist viewpoint during a period of Irish history when nationalist sentiment was on the increase. The ISRP put the cause of labour and the political needs of the Irish working class to the forefront of its politics, and as such should hold a special place in the history of the Irish labour movement. Its emphasis on social justice for the working class, its opposition to what it saw as the pernicious effects of capitalism on those who work under it and its strong internationalism, combined with a principled stand against imperialism, both in Ireland and abroad make the politics espoused by the ISRP still very relevant to the radical political tradition in modern Ireland.

Finally, a note on terminology. Throughout this study there are references to 'advanced nationalist' groups and individuals. Connolly used the phrase himself to distinguish between those nationalists of the more militant and separatist kind and the conservative Home Rule Party. Connolly also sometimes called these groups 'revolutionary nationalist' or 'republicans'. Most historians use the term in a broad sense to cover political groups such as Sinn Féin, individuals such as Arthur Griffith and cultural organisations such as the Gaelic League and the GAA. That is how the term is used in this study.

NOTES

1. James Connolly, *A Rebel Song*, published in Helen Clarke *Sing a Rebel Song The Story of James Connolly* (Edinburgh: City of Edinburgh District Council and Irish History Workshop, 1989).
2. Trotsky, quoted in Tony Cliff, *Lenin 1917–23: Revolution Besieged* (London: Bookmarks, 1987), p. 4. Trotsky was addressing the Menshevik members of the Central Soviet who had walked out of the chamber in protest at the establishment of the Bolshevik government after the October Revolution in Russia in 1917.
3. See Donal McCartney (ed.), *Parnell: The Politics of Power* (Dublin: Wolfhound Press, 1991).
4. F.S.L. Lyons, *Ireland Since the Famine* (London: Fontana Press, 1985), p. 270.

5. See Padraig Yates, *Lockout Dublin 1913* (Dublin: Gill and Macmillan, 2000), Conor Kostick, *Popular Militancy in Ireland 1917–23* (London: Pluto Press, 1997), Liam Cahill, *Forgotten Revolution: The Limerick Soviet 1919* (Cork: O'Brien Press, 1991), Fintan Lane, *The Origins of Modern Irish Socialism 1881–1896* (Cork: Cork University Press, 1997).
6. Benedict Anderson, *Imagined Communities: Reflections on the Origin and Spread of Nationalism* (London: Verso, 1991).
7. Sean Cronin, *Young Connolly* (Dublin: Repsol, 1983).
8. Peter Berresford Ellis, *A History of the Irish Working Class* (London: Pluto Press, 1996), pp. 173–5.
9. Samuel Levenson, *James Connolly: Socialist, Patriot and Martyr* (London: Quartet, 1977), p. 44.
10. Emmett O'Connor, *A Labour History of Ireland 1824–1960* (Cork: Cork University Press, 1992), p. 63.
11. See Lane, *The Origins of Modern Irish Socialism*, p. 214. Lane's study brilliantly chronicles in minute detail the early origins of socialist organisation on the island and he is at pains to show that the arrival of James Connolly to Dublin in early 1896 was not the 'big bang' moment in the origins of Irish socialism. This study generally agrees with Lane's view that the 'importance of the ISRP lay in the ideas of socialist republicanism rather than in organisational factors' (*Origins* , p. 3). Other organisations existed on the left in Ireland before 1896, but the ISRP represents such a profound political break from what went before that it is clearly the true pioneer of the modern socialist and republican movement in Ireland. Numerous historians have agreed with this central point: the ISRP was 'in the long term an important watershed in the historical development of Irish socialism': W.K. Anderson, *James Connolly and the Irish Left* (Dublin: Irish Academic Press, 1994), p. 51; the foundation of the ISRP by James Connolly 'was to carve out a tradition of politics that has had a major influence on the Irish left ever since:' Kieran Allen, *The Politics of James Connolly* (London: Pluto Press, 1990), p.13. 'It was Connolly who founded the Irish Socialist Republican Party; the first republican and the first socialist party in Ireland:' Proinsias Mac Aonghusa, *What Connolly Said* (Dublin: New Island Books, 1995), pp. 10–11: 'Its successes [the ISRP's] were few, but its posthumous influence was considerable. Connolly hoped to build Socialism in Ireland on a Fenian base': Cronin, *Young Connolly*, p. 31.
12. Thomas Johnson, *Irish Labour and its International Relations in the Era of the Second International and the Bolshevik Revolution* (Cork: Cork Workers Club, 1975), p. 37.
13. James Connolly, 'Introduction', *Erin's Hope* (New York: 1909), p. 2 (publisher unknown).
14. William O'Brien, *Forth the Banners Go* (Dublin: Three Candles, 1969), p. 4.

CHAPTER ONE

The Early Years, 1896–98

PRELUDE TO THE ISRP

A purely socialist movement cannot be expected in Ireland for a considerable time. People there want first of all to become peasants owning a plot of land, and after they have achieved that mortgages will appear on the scene and they will be ruined once more.
– Frederick Engels in an interview in the
New Yorker Volkszeitung, 20 September 1888

Eight years after Karl Marx's political partner Engels poured cold water on the prospects of any socialist party growing in Ireland, James Connolly and his comrades in the Irish Socialist Republican Party (ISRP) set out to attempt just that. Yet despite the high hopes that Connolly had for his political project in 1896, there is little doubt that the pessimistic note sounded by Engels about the immediate future of socialism in late-nineteenth-century Ireland had more than a ring of truth to it. Ireland in 1896 was a product of the major changes that had occurred in the country in the previous decades, in particular the Great Famine, and these changes had left a poor soil for socialism.

The movement of history can sometimes seem like the slow creeping process of glacial shifts, with nothing more than tiny microscopic changes taking place. Then, apparently out of nowhere a volcanic eruption can completely revolutionise the topology of the present and make the past seem almost like a foreign county. The social philosophy of Marxism also has a view on this pattern of historical change. Marxism sees small movements on a microscopic level leading to large revolutionary historical change on the broader, 'macro' level. History for the Marxist is marked by constant movement, a movement that is dialectical in nature, meaning that the pace of change is fuelled by the contradictions and conflicts in society. This is the view of history, as dialectical and materialist, that James Connolly held.

In the years before the Great Famine in Ireland (1845–48) the slow development in Ireland's social structure and agriculture created the material basis for the horrific outcome.[1] Writing in the early months of the ISRP Connolly described the years of the Great Famine as the 'blackest period of Ireland's history' and he further described the actions of the leaders of 'national Ireland' of the period as that which could be read only in the 'page of a comic opera'.[2] However, as a student of the nineteenth-century German socialist Karl Marx, Connolly did not blame the British government *per se* for the disaster. In his own central work, *Labour in Irish History*, Connolly pointed the finger of blame firmly at the economic system of capitalism for the mass starvation and emigration that resulted from those years. It was the economic system, rather than the subjective decisions taken by the individual members of the British government that was in the final analysis the central reason for the 'great hunger'.

> No man who accepts capitalist society and the laws thereof can logically find fault with the statesmen of England for their acts in that awful period. They stood for the rights of property and free competition, and philosophically they accepted their consequences upon Ireland; the leaders of the Irish people also stood for the rights of property, and refused to abandon them even when they saw their consequences in the slaughter by famine of over a million of the toilers.[3]

The Famine looms large over the final decades of the nineteenth century in Ireland: it set in motion a series of social changes that created the society in which the ISRP tried to grow from 1896 onwards. The political and physical landscape of Ireland changed dramatically during the second half of the nineteenth century. As Karl Marx noted, in the decade between 1855 and 1866, 1,032,694 Irishmen were replaced on the land by 996,877 head of livestock.[4] In the wake of the horrific devastation caused by the Great Famine, land use in Ireland witnessed a major shift towards pasture. By 1903, 81 per cent of the country was under pasture.[5] As the men and women chased away by hunger left the land they did not have major cities to find work in on the island. Unlike the labour surplus in the British countryside, which had moved into the burgeoning industrial towns in northern England in the late eighteenth and early nineteenth centuries, the rural Irish population headed for the emigration ships destined for the United States and elsewhere. Those who were starved off the land had to look abroad as urban Ireland offered little in the way of opportunity. Ireland's cities, particularly Dublin, reflected the island's economic subservient colonial relationship with Great Britain. In Dublin in 1901 only 21 per cent of the male workforce and 24.5 per cent of the total workforce was engaged in manufacturing; 44 per cent of women in Dublin were employed in domestic labour while almost 18 per cent of men were described as 'general labourers'.[6] Ireland was destined to be the supplier of agricultural raw materials to Britain by the second half of the nineteenth century. In this case raw materials principally meant meat.

With the Irish countryside going through such major changes, coupled with the underdevelopment of any industrial base apart from the northern city of Belfast, Ireland in 1896 was always going to be a difficult place to build a revolutionary socialist organisation. Ireland's economy was marked by its economic relationship with Great Britain, a relationship that led to industrial backwardness and underdevelopment on the island.

Belinda Probert argues in *Beyond Orange and Green* that the uneven development of capitalism in Ireland made political division along nationalist and unionist lines, and later partition, possible. Following the uneven historical development of industry on the island, Probert argues that the differences between the semi-capitalistic mode of production in the Belfast region and the general economic backwardness of the rest of the island can be traced as far back as the differing nature of the 'plantations' that took place in the sixteenth and seventeenth centuries. The final plantation that occurred in Ulster, in contrast to the plantations in the other three provinces in the sixteenth and seventeenth centuries, sowed the social seeds needed for capitalism to develop:

> It was only in the province of Ulster that England's policy of establishing control through 'plantation' had any success, with significant numbers of English and particularly Scots Presbyterian settlers taking over the land. The remaining three provinces of Ireland were still overwhelmingly dependent on agriculture, with political and economic power firmly in the hands of the great English landlords.[7]

By the mid-nineteenth century the mode of production in the northern urban areas, principally Belfast, was fundamentally different from that of the south. The linen and shipbuilding industries in the north were very strong, while by the end of the nineteenth century the economy in the rest of Ireland was almost completely agricultural, based on grazing farms rather than the smaller tillage holdings that had marked the countryside before the Great Famine. The retarded development of capitalism in Ireland was a result of its role within the British Empire. Kieran Allen argues that the underdevelopment of Irish capitalism had little to do with the 'peculiar psychological' weakness of the indigenous Irish capitalist class, as some historians have suggested, rather:

> The problem arose from the relationship between Ireland and the British Empire. The colonisation of Ireland by Britain led to the breaking down of many pre-capitalist tribal structures. The cash nexus, the market and petty commodity production were established quicker than they would have had colonisation not occurred. But the strength of the British economy and the intervention of the British state on its behalf ensured that the Irish economy was shaped in British interests.[8]

Ireland's political subjection and its economic problems in the nineteenth century were issues that Karl Marx and the First International (the worldwide organisation representing socialist parties) were very much interested in. Marx worked closely with the Irish Fenian leadership and was a supporter of the cause of freedom in Ireland. James Stephens, one of the leading members of the militant Irish Republican Brotherhood (IRB), was a convinced socialist and a member of the First International, and was influenced by Marx himself. The concern that Marx and his collaborator Frederick Engels gave to Ireland can be seen in the 500 pages of tight text dealing with the political and social problems of the island that fill their *Collected Works.*[9] Engels visited Ireland and attempted to learn Gaelic to help him write the history of the Irish that he had only begun before he died in 1895. Marx recognised that British domination of the island had led to the underdevelopment of the Irish economy. He claimed that 'every time Ireland was about to develop industrially, she was crushed and re-converted into a purely agricultural land'.[10] Both Marx and Engels viewed the issue of Ireland essentially through the political problems faced by the British labour movement. In one sense this was understandable. Britain was the centre of the industrial world, with the most developed and class-conscious proletariat.

However, it is interesting to contrast Marx's justification for defending the right of Ireland to self-determination in the 1860s with that of the ISRP three decades later. The ISRP viewed independence as essential to any political progress by the Irish working class. It united the call for a free and independent Ireland with the establishment of a Workers' Republic. The ISRP tackled the 'Irish Question' from the viewpoint of the political needs of the Irish working class, not from the perspective or through the prism of the British labour movement.

Although Marx had great sympathy for, and interest in, the plight of Ireland, he viewed the 'Irish Question' from the starting point of the political needs of the English proletariat, whom he believed to be of crucial importance to the cause of international socialism. Marx argued that any successful socialist revolution in England would be sparked off in Ireland and he proposed two principal reasons for this. First, he regarded the income from Irish rents paid to English landlords as an important economic bulwark protecting the English landed aristocracy from a growing and militantly class-conscious proletariat in their own country:

> In the first place, Ireland is the bulwark of English landlordism. If it fell in Ireland it would fall in England. In Ireland this is a hundred times easier since the economic struggle there is concentrated exclusively on landed property, since this struggle is at the same time national, and since the people there are more revolutionary and exasperated than in England. Landlordism in Ireland is maintained solely by the English army. The moment the forced union between the two countries ends, a social revolution will immediately break out in Ireland, though in outmoded forms. English landlordism would not only lose a great source of wealth, but also its greatest moral force, i.e., that of representing the domination of England over Ireland. On the other hand, by maintaining the power of their landlords in Ireland, the English proletariat makes them invulnerable in England itself.[11]

The emphasis that Marx placed on the rents collected from the Irish by the English land-owning class was proved by history to be overestimated. Just a few short years after Marx wrote this the British government began the slow but deliberate transfer of land from the large British landlords to the Irish peasantry through numerous Land Acts. As Chris Bambery has written: 'The diminishing importance of Irish rents for the maintenance of the British ruling class was demonstrated by Gladstone's ability to transfer most of the Anglo-Irish estates to the Catholic peasantry.'[12]

The second reason why Marx believed the 'Irish Question' to be of central importance to the prospects of socialism in Britain was the presence of a large number of Irish workers in English cities by the 1860s. Forced to emigrate after the Famine, these workers often worked for lower wages than their English counterparts and competed for the small number of jobs on offer:

> ...the English bourgeoisie has not only exploited the Irish poverty to keep down the working class in England by forced immigration of poor Irishmen, but it has also divided the proletariat into two hostile camps. The revolutionary fire of the Celtic worker does not go well with the nature of the Anglo-Saxon worker, solid, but slow. On the contrary, in all the big industrial centres in England there is profound antagonism between the Irish proletariat and the English proletariat. The average English worker hates the Irish worker as a competitor who lowers wages and the standard of life. He feels national and religious antipathies for him. He regards him somewhat like the poor whites of the Southern States of North America regard their black slaves. This antagonism among the proletarians of England is artificially nourished and supported by the bourgeoisie. It knows that this scission is the true secret of maintaining its power.[13]

The resentment felt by English workers towards Irish workers led to a potential political paralysis in the wider labour movement. This deep division between the native English and the Irish proletariat, particularly in the industrial towns of Lancashire, served the English ruling class well by creating schisms among workers and preventing maximum unity within the labouring class in Great Britain.

This approach of the First International and Karl Marx towards the 'Irish Question' serves only to highlight the major theoretical rupture represented by the political programme of the ISRP, and the significant differences between that party's rationale for fighting for an independent Ireland and that of earlier socialists including Karl Marx.

The urban areas of Ireland in which the ISRP tried to build were not the most advantageous foundation on which to construct a socialist organisation. By 1891 Belfast had outstripped Dublin in terms of population, and the country's capital was suffering from poverty and frequent outbreaks of disease. Dublin had one of the highest death rates in the world and this mortality rate was a major election issue when the ISRP stood in local elections, in 1899 and in later years. Only 17,755 males worked in manufacturing employment in Dublin in

1901. Of these 2,472 worked in 'food and drinks' – essentially brewing, a sign of the importance of Guinness as a central focus for the employment of large numbers of workers in Dublin at the time.[14] Many of these working in manufacturing were general labourers. General labourers tended to be unskilled workers whom the craft workers in Dublin greatly feared. The craft unions were tightly knit closed shops, as the high level of unemployment caused by the Famine and the migration of rural dwellers to Dublin meant that jobs were at a premium, and those who had the skills did not want the unemployed moving into their sector. Dublin was also a city marked by the hold that British imperialism had over it. It was an important port in the workings of the British Empire, but the majority of its citizens lived a life of grinding poverty.

Yet these urban issues were not what dominated the politics of the time. The individual socialists and the small socialist groups active in Ireland before 1896 rarely if ever made any impact on the wider political agenda, and were almost completely isolated from public political discourse.[15] The fight for Home Rule and the continuing 'Land War' were the major political themes of the early 1890s. This changed late in the decade, when a period of political and cultural renewal saw many young artists, writers and people interested in progressive politics forming social, political and cultural groups in the urban centres. This radical milieu became known as the 'Gaelic Revival'.

Before the arrival of the ISRP the socialist movement had had a rather fitful and enigmatic history. In the early 1890s the British Independent Labour Party (ILP) established branches up and down the county. These branches were established after James Keir Hardie, who was the leading light in the British labour movement and the future founder of the British Labour Party, had travelled across Ireland in an attempt to establish a foothold for socialism. By 1896 the ILP branch in Dublin had ceased to exist and its remnants had re-formed into a loose group called the Dublin Socialist Society. The leading members of this society were Robert Dorman and Adolphus Shiels. Both men had been involved in the Irish socialist scene for many years. Dorman held weekly outdoor propaganda meetings on the streets of Dublin; Shiels was the secretary of the society and was also a member of the Fabian Society.[16] The Dublin Socialist Society was a very loose organisation that allowed socialists of various types to join and did not stick to any strict internal structure. It was this group that was to answer the advertisement promoting the talents of a socialist organiser in *Justice*, the newspaper of the British Social Democratic Federation (SDF) in late 1895.[17] The advertisement flagged the abilities of a 27-year-old socialist organiser from Edinburgh named James Connolly. The Scottish socialist John Leslie wrote highly of Connolly's abilities as a socialist organiser in the advertisement.

> I may say that very few men have I met deserving of greater love and respect than James Connolly, he is the most able propagandist in every sense of the word that Scotland has turned out.[18]

By the time that the small group of Dublin socialists read the advertisement, Connolly had been active in the socialist movement in Scotland for seven years. He was born in 1868 in the predominantly Catholic Irish Cowgate area of Edinburgh, to Irish working-class parents. Having spent time in Ireland serving in the British Army, Connolly joined the socialist movement in Scotland in 1889 after fleeing his regiment. The Edinburgh-based socialist John Leslie, author of *The Present Position of the Irish Question*, exerted a huge influence on the young Connolly, and Leslie's pamphlet was one of the first to be printed by the ISRP. In this pamphlet Leslie makes political arguments similar to those that were to be developed by Connolly later, principally on the important role that the Irish working class had to play in the fight for Irish freedom:

> It is none other than the wage-earners of town and country who have fought the Irish fights since '48, and who have furnished nine-tenths of the martyrs and victims of the fight, without reaping any of the advantages that may have followed from it.[19]

Leslie was the first secretary of the Scottish Socialist Federation (SSF), formed in 1889. This was an organisation that attempted to unite all the various socialist groupings in Edinburgh at the time. The main Marxist party active in Edinburgh in the 1890s was the SDF, led by the intellectual Henry Hyndman. The other major socialist grouping in Scotland was the more reformist and less radical ILP, led by Keir Hardie. Although Connolly was for a period a member of the ILP, eventually it was the brand of revolutionary socialism preached by the SDF that influenced him most before he left for Ireland in 1896.[20]

Connolly was secretary of the SSF for a time and was also a socialist organiser for a number of different leftist groups. Twice he stood unsuccessfully as a socialist candidate in local elections in Edinburgh in the 1890s. A person who was so openly a socialist found it hard to find work and after a prolonged period of unemployment Connolly resolved to leave Scotland. A move to South America was briefly flirted with, but in the end the response from Dublin to the advertisement in *Justice* came at just the right time in Connolly's life and he travelled to Dublin in early 1896 to meet his new employers.

'SIX WORKING MEN ASSISTED AT ITS BIRTH'

According to Connolly there were only six men sitting in Pierce Ryan's pub on Thomas Street, Dublin, on 29 May 1896, when the Dublin Socialist Society was reconstituted as the Irish Socialist Republican Party (ISRP) with Connolly as full-time organiser. However, notwithstanding the usual tendency of political activists to overestimate the number of people in attendance at organised events, it seems that Connolly may actually have underestimated, ever so slightly, the size of that first meeting.[21] Whatever the exact number in attendance at the meeting in Ryan's, it is true to say that the party began with a small base and that the problems associated with building its membership were to dog the organisation for the next eight years. Having just arrived in Ireland a few weeks before, Connolly was approved as full-time Secretary at a weekly wage of one pound at that first meeting. Because of the financial problems suffered by the party, this wage was not always paid and Connolly often had to do some part-time work to make up the shortfall. Tom Lyng was elected Party Treasurer; as this was a part-time post, he was not paid. The other members known to have been in attendance at that first meeting were Robert Dorman, Murtagh Lyng, John Moore, Patrick Cushan, Alex Kennedy and Peter Kavanagh.[22]

Connolly, as the party's full-time officer, got down to work almost instantaneously and the newly formed party set about arranging a gruelling timetable of summer season educational meetings. These were held as outdoor public meetings, normally either in Foster Place, beside the Bank of Ireland on College Green, or in the Phoenix Park on Sunday evenings at 7.30 pm.

The party was officially launched at a public meeting at the Custom House, Dublin, on 7 June 1896. Alexander Blane, who had been a Home Rule MP on the Parnellite wing, chaired the first meeting, but he never became a member of the organisation. Blaine's presence showed his own close ties to the labour movement – he had developed some close connections with the British socialist William Morris in London in the late 1880s – but it also suggests how the ISRP viewed the pro-Parnell wing of the split Home Rule Party: as the more progressive rump of the remnants of that organisation.

Later in the year public meetings were held indoors, in a hall on Marlborough Street. Some members eventually came to believe that these meetings were becoming too sedate and thus it was decided in October 1898 that the meetings would be 'enlivened by music and revolutionary songs' in an attempt to attract more people, and to bring some passion to the proceedings.[23]

The introductory entrance fee to join the party was set at six (old) pence, while the minimum weekly subscription for party members was one penny. The original offices of the party were at 67 Middle Abbey Street in Dublin, but the party was to make a number of moves during the years. In September 1899 the party moved down the street to number 138; two years later, in March 1902, it moved to offices at 6 Lower Liffey Street. The party's first office, in the heart of Dublin city centre, was very rudimentary when it came to furniture. According to one party member, William O'Brien, the cramped rooms had a hand press, a couple of cases that held the type, a 'dingy table', three or four benches and one chair without a back 'for the Secretary'. It was in these modest surroundings that the ISRP attempted to begin a revolution in Ireland, to establish socialism and in Connolly's tongue-in-cheek words, to precipitate the 'incidental destruction of the British Empire'.

Apart from Connolly the principal propagandists inside the ISRP were Murtagh Lyng and his brother Tom, Edward W. Stewart, Daniel O'Brien, Thomas O'Brien, William O'Brien, Con O'Lyhane, William McLoughlin and William Bradshaw.

The Lyng brothers were from County Kildare and had been active socialists in Ireland for a few years before Connolly's arrival. In 1893 both brothers visited Liverpool and came under the influence of Kier Hardie's ILP. When they returned to Ireland they attempted to help to build an ILP branch in Dublin. Both men became strong supporters of Connolly. Murtagh, in particular, grew in confidence as a socialist speaker and writer, and Lyng eventually became the editor of the *Workers' Republic* in later years, when Connolly was abroad on fund-raising speaking trips. Tom was a shop assistant in Dublin and worked in various stores during his years in the ISRP. Murtagh, like a number of the ISRP's members, worked for Dublin Corporation. He was employed as a sanitary inspector, not the most appealing job at the best of times, and Dublin's inner-city slums in 1896, where Murtagh spent much of his time, were far from the best of places. This constant exposure to the daily drudgery of proletarian life in the slums of Dublin fuelled Muratgh's strong sense of the need for social justice.

The O'Briens were the other set of brothers who made a major impact on the internal life of the ISRP. The O'Briens hailed from Clonakilty in County Cork, but the family had moved to Dublin when the three brothers were very young. Dan O'Brien was a brilliant writer and one of the most active members of the party. He was one of the best speakers in the ISRP and was a regular contributor to the public meetings organised by the party. He had a particular interest in health issues and how they affected the Dublin working class. William was the youngest O'Brien brother and was too young to join the organisation in 1896: he eventually joined in 1899 (surprisingly, it was Tom Lyng, rather than either of his brothers who recruited him). William was a master tailor and represented his trade at various levels of his union, the Amalgamated Society of Tailors. William was also a great collector of documents, letters, papers and resolutions. It is on his papers, now available in the National Library of Ireland (NLI), that much of Irish labour history has been based, including this study. William became fiercely loyal to Connolly in later years and became Connolly's literary executor after Francis Sheehy Skeffington, Connolly's original choice, was killed in 1916. Although William was very close to Connolly after the split in the ISRP, during the existence of the party he was not afraid to disagree openly with Connolly. Indeed, William sided with the anti-Connolly faction within the party in 1903. In the decades before his death in 1968, William was to go on to become one of the most important figures in the Irish labour movement.

Con O'Lyhane was the colourful and brash ISRP organiser in Cork. Young, energetic and with a strong grasp of socialist politics, O'Lyhane attempted for many months to help the ISRP to sink real roots in the Cork area. He was born in Coachford, County Cork, in 1877 and, while living and working in the 'rebel city', he was to clash regularly with Connolly over issues of party policies. After leaving the party O'Lyhane was to have a significant involvement in both British and American left-wing movements.

William McLoughlin was a Dublin tailor who represented his trade in the Dublin craft unions. He was one of the most influential members of the ISRP in the trade union movement.

William Bradshaw was almost like a press officer in the early years of the ISRP. Another strong admirer of Connolly, Bradshaw consistently kept in touch with the mainstream press in Dublin to let them know of upcoming meetings and other party events.

Edward Stewart, a Dublin man, joined the party in late 1896 and was to make an impact on the organisation surpassed only by that of Connolly himself. Stewart had been a tailor, but while he was a member of the party he became a warehouse assistant in a major tailoring establishment in Dublin. A tireless worker in the early years, Stewart was the ISRP's first election candidate. Deeply involved in Dublin's trade union circles, Stewart was elected President of the Dublin Trades Council in September 1902 – the most significant union post held by any member of the ISRP. After this Stewart's politics took a sharp turn to the right and he was to become a major thorn in Connolly's side in the final months of the ISRP.[24]

Other faces on the political left in Dublin joined the party in the early months, only to leave very soon afterwards. Robert Dorman was in attendance at the very first meeting in Ryan's and even proposed the motion to reconstitute the Dublin Socialist Society as the ISRP. However, Dorman moved to Limerick later in 1896 and it seems that his ties with the party began to come under some strain. Not interested in building a branch of the ISRP in Limerick, believing that there was little audience for the party in the area, but coming under pressure from the Dublin-based leadership to build a branch nonetheless, Dorman tendered his resignation on 17 June 1897.[25] The party in Dublin accepted it unanimously. Just over twelve months after inviting Connolly to come to Dublin, Dorman had severed his links with the organisation. Maybe Dorman's strong evangelical Protestant beliefs had led to some problems with the mainly Catholic party leadership. Dorman did not retire from politics and continued to preach his brand of Christian socialism after he moved to Belfast. Adolphus Shields, the other man who invited Connolly to Ireland, also joined the ISRP briefly in the early months, but it seems that he returned to his Fabian roots and never became fully involved in the party.[26] These men, who had been socialist activists in Dublin during the decades before Connolly's arrival, may have found the new thinking, new direction and new energy that Connolly undoubtedly brought to the socialist scene in Ireland a little hard to live with.

Despite these early resignations, the party quickly fell into a rhythm of weekly activity built around meetings dealing with internal party matters. The weekly meetings, referred to as 'business meetings' by the members, normally took place in the party offices every Monday at 8.30 pm. Detailed minutes of these meetings were kept. The meetings were not always well-attended and it was noted as early as 1898 by some of the more reliable party stalwarts that there was a continuing problem of 'very small attendance of members'.[27] The meetings were essentially attended by the Dublin-based active membership of the party, with the few members that the organisation had outside the Dublin region rarely travelling to the capital. As William O'Brien later noted: 'If 18 turned up it would be looked on almost as a mass meeting.'[28] At the beginning of each meeting the minutes from the previous week would be read out and voted on. Written correspondence, of which there was a surprisingly large amount, was then read to the membership. Most of the post came from socialist groups in North America and Europe: the ISRP got little in the way of letters from within Ireland. Then the party would discuss the topic for their next open public meeting and the major political issues of the day.

The ISRP quickly grew into a party of tens of members rather than just the handful of original founders and became very distinctive on the Dublin political scene. One party member rather fondly remembered how Connolly had won over the small number of socialists involved with the Dublin Socialist Society to his line of thinking as he 'pulverised them in debate, shattered their little organisation and from the fragments founded the small Irish Socialist Republican Party'.[29]

In reality, the active membership of the ISRP never surpassed eighty, although the number of people who had some association with the organisation or who joined even for a short period between 1896 and 1904 probably reached a few hundred. Austen Morgan has declared that the party was 'of course, a sect on the extremity of Dublin politics' but this description is unfair.[30] The term 'sect' has connotations of a small organisation interested primarily in its own internal life and unwilling to engage with the realities or the people inhabiting the outside world. The ISRP always showed a great deal of willingness to engage with the wider political scene in Dublin and attempted, through hundreds of public meetings and the publication of volumes of literature, to push its politics among the general public.

The younger members of the party became well-known for sporting long hair and were seen as rather 'bohemian' for the Dublin of the period. This bohemian image led to some friction between the party and the wider trade union movement, which was both

politically and socially very conservative. While most of the members were 'workers', the party was not mainly 'recruited from the industrial working class', although much of the reason for this can be traced to the relatively small size of the industrial working class in Dublin.[31] Yet the youthful nature of the organisation was always a source of pride for Connolly. When looking at the changes in the electoral system in 1899, Connolly confidently predicted that more and more young men would vote at election time – the very sort who were attracted to the politics of the ISRP:

> Then each year will see the addition to the roll of voters of more and more votes from the ranks of young men on whom the full effect of our propaganda is primarily felt.[32]

The party held public meetings that frequently drew large crowds both in the Phoenix Park and at Foster Place. Whether all the people who gathered to hear Connolly and his comrades speaking were seriously there for the politics, or were just intrigued by the spectacle, is, of course, difficult to judge. The party took these meetings very seriously, and sold literature and, later, its own paper among the crowds that gathered. The meetings dealt with points of socialist theory, with the ISRP's speakers attempting to popularise the theories of 'scientific socialism' to a Dublin audience that had little experience of such politics. The open-air meetings, particularly at Foster Place – a city centre location – were sometimes very well-attended and police officers were often seen patrolling the perimeters of the crowd. Yet the meetings were also at the mercy of the Irish weather and could be completely washed out at very short notice. Hecklers also disturbed the meetings and sometimes the odd scuffle broke out at the fringes of the gathering. In attempting to organise such large-scale public meetings with such a small membership the ISRP often ran into difficulties. The party's minutes contain a detailed account of one meeting that went wrong.

Daniel O'Brien was to speak on the topic of 'Reform or Revolution' to an audience in a hall at 67 Marlborough Street:

> At 8 pm there was a very good attendance of members and outside public, who patiently waited for the lecturer to materialise. About 8.45 it was discovered that this gentleman [Daniel O'Brien] was in bed, presumably sick. Stewart thereon filled the gap and lectured on the same subject. He was mercilessly heckled over some analogies he drew from a public house in the course of his address.[33]

The party began to become very sophisticated when it came to the effective organisation of meetings. Indeed, Tom Lyng, proposed a motion at a business meeting that meant that members were 'recommended to mix with crowd previous to opening of meeting conversing on topics Socialistic'.[34] Many of the ISRP's members became quite well-known in a city where public speakers, who were virulently and openly anti-capitalist as well as anti-British, were not the norm:

> Once, when Connolly and Lyng went to Cole's Lane to buy a table, a little girl cried out: 'Oh Mother, look at Mr Chairman', pointing at Lyng. It was a kind of fame.[35]

The weekly public meeting dealt with topics such as the Paris Commune, 'Socialism and State Capitalism', 'The Technical Terms of Scientific Socialism: Their Meaning and Application', 'Collectivism and Democracy', 'Whether Capitalists are Honest or Necessary', 'Reform or Revolution' and 'Are We Utopians'.[36] The stress on educational meetings was something that Connolly had picked up from his days working with the SDF in Scotland. Individual members of the party were encouraged to speak at these forums, to help to heighten their own personal grasp of socialist politics as well as to build up their confidence as public speakers. The educational meetings finished in 1897[37] while larger public meetings continued, although the level of politics preached at these gatherings was of a more popular and less intricate and detailed nature. The cessation of the educational meetings was regretted by members of the party in the dying days of the organisation, when it was felt that the majority of party members no longer had a strong enough grasp and understanding of socialism. Many members saw their discontinuation as one of the reasons for this ideological and political deficit among members in the final months of the party.

Non-party speakers often addressed the public meetings. For example members of the Amalgamated Society of Railway Servants addressed the ISRP at a meeting on Sunday 27 March 1899 that closed with a rousing rendition of the 'Marseillaise'. In 1901 the party published in pamphlet form a lecture given by William Gallagher to the Cork Branch of the organisation entitled *Work, Wages and Profits*. Gallagher attended a number of meetings of the ISRP and eventually joined for a brief period. He had a university degree in economics and Connolly regarded him as a good speaker on socialist economic theory. After the collapse of the party Gallagher received an MA in economics and went to work for the Indian government in the Research Department in the Malay Peninsula.[38] The republican playwright Fred Ryan also addressed a number of ISRP meetings. Arthur Griffith gave an undertaking to Edward Stewart that he would address a meeting of the party on the topic of economics, but it seems that the future founder of Sinn Féin never got around to speaking before an ISRP gathering.

In 1896 the publication of a party paper was still two years away, but the ISRP made a decision early on to bring out a pamphlet containing works written by Fintan Lalor, one of the leading lights of the 'Young Ireland' movement of 1848. Connolly and the ISRP saw Lalor as standing for the more left-wing element of that movement. Lalor had looked to the poor peasantry as the agency for revolution, rather than the large landowners. In 1897 the ISRP decided to publish some of Lalor's writings before the commemoration of the centenary of the 1798 Rising, in an attempt to influence the debate surrounding the upcoming commemoration.

The party sold numerous other items of literature at these open-air meetings, such as *Wage Labour and Capital* by Karl Marx, *The Present Position of the Irish Question* by John Leslie, the pamphlet (already mentioned) that had a major influence on the thinking of the young Connolly. The party produced its own series of pamphlets, the first of which was published in late 1896. At least eight pamphlets were produced in the 'Workers' Republic Pamphlets' series, including *Public Health and Capitalism: Being the Report of a Lecture Delivered Before the Dublin Branch of the Irish Socialist Republican Party*, Daniel O'Brien.[39] Connolly's pamphlet *Erin's Hope* was the first to be published in the series, and, was also sold in Great Britain and the United States. The front cover of the pamphlets displayed a female figure representing Ireland holding a sword. On the sword was inscribed 'Educated Irish Democracy', bearing witness to the emphasis that the party placed on building up the intellectual levels of the party members and the wider proletariat as a precondition for socialism. The female figure is pointing at the setting sun in the far distance, with the words 'Socialist Republic' emblazoned upon the sun.

Con O'Lyhane, the Cork-based member of the party, designed the front cover of the pamphlet after some persuasion from his comrades. O'Lyhane was a bit of an artist having had a number of drawings published in the *Cork Examiner*.

Looking back in 1902 at the early months of the organisation's existence, Connolly described in great detail the problems faced by the ISRP in building a party in Ireland:

> The founders were poor, like the remainder of their class, and had arrayed against them all those things that are supposed to be essential to success. They were without a press of any kind, their propaganda was generally supposed to be hostile to the religious views of the majority of the people, no great or well-known name allied itself to them, they had to count on the bitter opposition of all the organised parties which defend the interests of the propertied class, their opponents had more sovereigns to spare for political work than they had coppers, they were in a country undeveloped industrially, and a country in which political freedom was not fully realised, and where, therefore, the political mission of Liberalism or middle-class reformers was not yet exhausted – in short, they were handicapped as no other party in this country ever yet were handicapped; hated by the government, held in distrust by the people, and in short generally regarded as Ishmaels in the political life of Ireland.
>
> But that little band of pioneers stuck to their work manfully, and despite all discouragements and rebuffs continued sowing the seeds of Socialist working-class revolt in the furrows of discontent ploughed by the capitalist system of society. Today they can look back on their work with pride.[40]

As was to be expected, the ISRP suffered from chronic financial problems that were to be a source of difficulty from its foundation until its collapse. With such a small membership the party was never going to raise enough money from subscriptions to finance its activities. With rent and printing costs to meet the party looked at numerous ways of raising cash. As we have seen, literature was sold at meetings, but this did not lead to the accruement of the required level of finance to run the party effectively. The party even contemplated selling tobacco on a large scale on the streets of Dublin in an attempt to fund the organisation. It was believed, principally among the smokers in the party, that a very handy profit could be made by buying cheap tobacco and then selling it on, but this proposal was never pursued.[41] At one stage the party also discussed the possibility of selling tea in Dublin to help raise cash.[42] In the end the party was never able to create a secure financial base on which to build the organisation, leaving it in a continual state of financial insecurity.

The principally young membership of the ISRP also took part in the social side of life, combining politics with leisure. Chess and draughts

were played in the ISRP's offices and the party organised a number
of social events, particularly around Christmas time. These social
occasions saw the party membership getting together outside politics
to enjoy a drink and some music, although Connolly, a militant
teetotaller, stayed well away from the alcoholic refreshments. A
typical example of such events was the Christmas Party advertised in
the *Workers' Republic* in December 1899:

> A festive reunion of the members and friends of the Dublin branch
> of the I.S.R.P. will be held in our Hall, 138 Upper Abbey Street, on
> Christmas Eve at 8 pm. Tickets, which are two shillings each, may
> be had from the Secretary.[43]

Because of the constant activity undertaken by the party in Dublin,
with both indoor and outdoor meetings, the ISRP was viewed from
the outside as much larger and more influential than in reality it was.
In the first volume of his *Autobiographies* entitled *Drums Under the
Windows*, the Irish socialist playwright Sean O'Casey describes
attending a large ISRP open meeting in the early days of the party,
where he got speaking to an ISRP member with a thick Dublin accent
called Tom Egan:

> –Who's the big-bodied man getting up to speak? asked a man of
> him as he passed displaying the pamphlets.
> – That's James Connolly, our secretary, an' if you knew all you
> should know, you'd know without askin'.
> – Secretary of what? asked Sean.
> – Aw, God, th' ignorance here's devastatin'! said Egan, giving a
> wryer twist to his melancholy mouth; Secretary of the Irish Socialist
> Republican Party, an' if you knew well all you should know, you
> wouldn't have t' ask, Penny each, *Socialism Made Easy*, be the
> renowned Socialist Leader, James Connolly.
> – It doesn't look to be a mighty force of a party, murmured Sean.
> – Aw, you count be numbers d'ye? And he looked with pitiful
> tolerance at Sean.[44]

While the party was beginning to build its profile in Dublin, it
failed to extend its influence across the country, although there were
numerous attempts to form branches outside the capital city. In late
September 1898 a proposal to form a branch of the party that would
hold fortnightly meetings among the Irish community in London was
also discussed but the branch never made a start.[45] Socialism was not
as strong among the Irish community in England as militant
nationalism or even the Home Rule Party.

Ernest Milligan (younger brother of the well-known Irish republican Alice Milligan, editor of the Fenian paper *Shan Van Vocht*) formed a branch in the same month in Belfast, the first meeting taking place in the Typographical Hall in that city on 10 September 1898.[46] This branch had a fleeting and fitful existence, coming under pressure from the Orange Order and being viewed with distrust by the socialists already active in Belfast as too 'pro-nationalist'. Alice Milligan never joined the ISRP, although she did invite Connolly to write a number of articles on socialist politics in her paper.

A Cork branch formed by Con O'Lyhane was also established in 1897. While this branch made some impact in the 'rebel city' it eventually came under intense pressure from the local clergy and disappeared.[47] The Cork branch, originally called 'The Fintan Lalor Club', was established to propagate 'the principles of Fintan Lalor and the Socialist Republican Party'. The use of Fintan Lalor's name in the title of the branch displayed in a practical sense how the ISRP intended to use figures from the more traditional nationalist historical 'canon' as part of their own political vision. This exemplifies the ISRP's attempts to create a bridgehead between its own socialism and the politics of the 'advanced' nationalists. This was how Connolly viewed the party from its very foundation: as the organisational link between the two traditions. He believed that the

> Irish question was at bottom an economic question, and that the economic struggle must be able to function nationally before it could function internationally, and as Socialists were opposed to all oppression so should they ever be foremost in the daily battle against all its manifestations, social and political. As the embodiment of this teaching, the party adopted the watchword, Irish Socialist Republic, and by deduction there from, the afore-mentioned name of their organisation.[48]

The party had small pockets of supporters in other areas of the country, such as Limerick and Waterford, but they failed to make a breakthrough in these cities. One ISRP member, Laurence Strange, attempted to form a branch in Waterford, but from early on he was very pessimistic about building the organisation in that city. Strange was a solicitor from Tramore who had founded a branch of the ILP in Waterford in 1894, when Keir Hardie visited the city. Strange had also been involved in the Home Rule movement, although he was always regarded as standing on the left wing of that party. Strange left the ISRP not long after its formation and he seems not to have been enamoured of the direction that Connolly was taking socialism in Ireland. Strange later rejoined the Home Rule organisation and actually became Mayor of Waterford representing that party. Predictably, he was unmercifully criticised in the pages of the *Workers' Republic* as a 'class traitor'.[49]

In October 1901 the party established a branch among Irish emigrants in Pendleton, Manchester, yet, true to form, this grouping lasted only for a few weeks.[50]

Despite these setbacks, in the early years Connolly was optimistic that the new party could witness some fairly rapid growth, believing that the disintegration of the Home Rule Party gave other political groupings opportunities to build their influence. Connolly was aware of the hold that Parnell had had over the Irish political scene before his own personal destruction. Parnell had skilfully created a pan-nationalist front, in the form of the 'New Departure', that for a time at least had held together the diverse political groupings in Ireland, as well as the Irish political community in the United States. For radicals in Ireland Parnell in his final months was a heroic figure, particularly after what is known as his 'Appeal to the Hillside', which was seen as a overt pitch for Fenian support.[51] However, like Wolfe Tone's famous call in 1798 to the 'Men of No Property' to rise up against the British, Parnell's appeal was more a threat to his own moderate supporters, who were turning their backs on him following Katherine O'Shea's divorce trial, than evidence of a true political conversion to militant republicanism. Despite his misgivings about much of Parnell's politics, Connolly believed that he was a progressive figure in Irish history, particularly when compared to the leadership of the Home Rule movement in the late 1890s. By 1896 Connolly also believed that, now that this major figure on the Irish political landscape had passed away, the Irish working class could be weaned away from support for the splintered Home Rulers, and in theory could be attracted by the politics of the ISRP:

> Meanwhile the manhood of Ireland, no longer dazzled by the glare of a great personality, have had their time to more closely examine their position, social and political. The working class of Ireland trusts no more the charming of the middle-class politician, strong in its own power it marches irresistibly forward to its destiny, the Socialist Republic.[52]

A number of individuals identified themselves with the party, while never agreeing wholeheartedly enough with the ISRP's political programme to become card-carrying members of the organisation. For example, the leading republican Maud Gonne actively campaigned alongside the party on the issue of the Boer War and, while she had a strong admiration for Connolly personally, she never joined the small group. In January 1897 Gonne wrote to the ISRP expressing her 'entire accord with the Republican and Socialist ideal of the party, but desiring an interview with the secretary [Connolly] before publicly identifying herself' with the ISRP. Connolly was never able to convince Gonne to join the party.[53]

The Irish republican and playwright Fred Ryan was also associated with the organisation and chaired a number of meetings. It seems that he did not approve of the general policy of the ISRP, although he did join the organisation for a short period.[54] Other political personalities on the scene, such as the republican writer Alice Milligan, expressed a general goodwill towards the party while never officially joining the ranks of the ISRP.

The party did attract interest from some notables in the international socialist movement. Eleanor Aveling, one of the daughters of Karl Marx, wrote a letter in support of the new organisation and her partner Edward Aveling became a member of the party.[55] This was a symbolic membership more than anything: Eleanor Aveling had supported the cause of Ireland and the Fenians for many years, and was deeply committed to the freedom of Ireland.

The ISRP never had a female member. The party was in favour of universal suffrage and through its programme called for equality for women, but the militant suffragette period was still a few years away, the question of women's rights was not yet centre-stage and the priorities of the ISRP reflected that. It could also be noted that the internal life of the ISRP was probably rather more attractive to men than to women in 1896 with card-playing and draughts over a few pints of stout forming the main focus of leisure activity for the members.

Because the party remained so small in membership, with few followers beyond the Greater Dublin region, the ISRP did not have to deal with some of the theoretical issues regarding the internal organisational structure of a revolutionary socialist party. While the issue was of great importance in other left-wing parties (particularly the Russian Social Democrat Workers' Party, which eventually split over an issue of party structure in 1903 into the Bolsheviks and Mensheviks), organisation and internal systems never concerned Connolly, or the party in general, all that much. However, Connolly did insist on the party taking detailed minutes at each meeting while also producing quarterly financial reports.

The party did not hold annual conferences or any regional delegated meetings. There were some standing posts, such as Secretary, which was almost always held by Connolly, and Treasurer, Financial Secretary, Literature Secretary and a Lecture Secretary, which were all held by the 'leading lights' of the ISRP at some stage. In 1902 there was even some mention of an Executive Committee of the organisation in party literature. Yet the ISRP was not organised along strict guidelines and lacked an internal constitution. The Secretary was seen as the 'important person', but there was no standing President. The idea of a party President was viewed as anti-democratic among members and at each of its weekly gatherings a new person was elected to preside as chairman over the business meetings. The minute-taker at each meeting was also frequently changed, something that is reflected in the wide range of handwriting styles and quality to be found in the ISRP's minute books that are still in existence. Connolly once gave a rather elaborate description of the internal organisation that in reality was based more on political aspiration than fact. According to Connolly, the party had

> no permanent president or chairman, thus avoiding the dangers of bossism and the perpetual intrigues for position which disgrace every other party. They recognise no person as leader, the most prominent speaker or writer has no more sway in the organisation than the most silent worker, they allow no party manifesto or leaflet to be signed by an individual, and thus no member can obtrude his personality upon the party, they insist on a regular system of book-keeping and a weekly statement and quarterly audit of all monies received and expended, thus giving every man a full knowledge of the party's actions, and finally they transact all business at weekly meetings in which every member is invited to take part. A party built upon such lines has no need of leaders nor yet has it any fear of them, aiming at a system of society that will be the embodiment of the principles of the fullest democracy alike in politics and industry.[56]

In hindsight there are a number of interesting ironies arising from this particular description of the ISRP's internal life. First, Connolly himself was the 'most prominent speaker or writer' within the party and he undoubtedly had 'more sway' in the party than most. This can be accounted for by the vast amount of time and effort that Connolly invested in the organisation, and his own theoretical grasp of socialism, which was at a much higher level than that of any of his party colleagues. The pronouncement that the party was free from 'bossism' is interesting, considering that this was to be the very charge levelled at Connolly by his enemies during the major split in the ISRP in 1903.

Second, the emphasis that Connolly places on the party having proper financial management is also worth focusing on, considering that financial 'irregularities' became one of the major points of disagreement among the party's members in the dying days of the organisation. Despite the description of the party given here by Connolly, the ISRP never developed any detailed blueprint for how a revolutionary organisation should organise itself. While Connolly often used words such as 'organised' or 'discipline', comparing the party to the 'pioneers' of the labour movement or the militant section of the mass 'army of labour', the ISRP was anything but tightly regimented. Although Connolly did have what could be described as a 'vanguard' notion of the party, as the organised expression of the most militant section of the working class leading the way towards socialism, in truth the party was often marked by internal anarchy rather than discipline. Thus a quarterly report of the party in April 1899 complains of the lack of professionalism shown by the ISRP's officers, with the noted exception of Connolly:

> In conclusion, we strongly recommend that a serious effort be made by officials during coming quarter to conduct the affairs of the organisation in a more systematic fashion than has been done. As far as the experience of the present auditors has gone, there has been nothing like a satisfactory effort on the part of the officials (excepting the Secretary) to do this.[57]

There were a few expulsions in the early years of the party, but it was not until the difficult period in 1903 that expulsions became a much more significant part of the ISRP's life. At one stage Connolly wanted to form a 'Re-organising Committee' to deal with the problem of the lack of effort shown by some of the ISRP's membership. In March 1899 the party had a detailed discussion regarding the general problems involved with internal discipline:

> A discussion took place upon the laxity of discipline which seems to be increasing among the members of the party and finally Connolly gave notice that at next meeting we would move that a reorganising committee be appointed.[58]

Nothing much changed internally for the party after the creation of the committee. If the party had grown larger, to include branches and members from across the 32 counties in Ireland, Connolly and the party might have had to consider a more coherent and developed vision of party organisation. As it was, the internal life of the party remained populated by a small number of active socialists

Thus the legacy of the ISRP lies not so much in the actual activity undertaken by the organisation but rather in its theoretical standpoint. The programme agreed upon by the party not long after the organisation's first meeting was the central plank of the party's political philosophy.

THE ISRP'S PROGRAMME, 1896

The ISRP programme, finalised in 1896, was to remain the organisation's central document of policy and aims. The programme was never altered, and was printed in full in every edition of the *Workers' Republic* from 1898 until 1903. Connolly drafted the document and it was passed by a few members of the party lying on the grass in St Stephen's Green, Dublin.[59]

The programme opens with one of Connolly's favourite quotations, Demouslins's aphorism 'The great appear great because we are on our knees: let us rise.' The document then goes on to describes the 'object' that the ISRP was aiming to achieve:

> Establishment of AN IRISH SOCIALIST REPUBLIC based upon the public ownership by the Irish people of the land, and instruments of production, distribution and exchange. Agriculture to be administered as a public function, under boards of management elected by the agricultural population and responsible to them and to the nation at large. All other forms of labour necessary to the well-being of the community to be conducted on the same principles.[60]

This short paragraph hardly gives a detailed account of how a future socialist society in Ireland would function, but the ISRP was no different than the majority of European socialist parties when it came to this lack of a clear blueprint for the future. The ISRP would have contended, just like Karl Marx himself, that it was not up to socialists to decide the exact outline of a future socialist society: rather, it was for the future ruling proletariat to decide democratically how socialism should function.

However, the ISRP did outline the broad political and economic parameters that it believed a future Irish Socialist Republic would work within. It is clear from what was written by the ISRP in other articles and pamphlets, as well as in the pages of the *Workers' Republic*, that the future Irish Workers' Republic would not just be free from the British Empire, but would also have a high level of state control over the economy. This state control would be coupled with an active democracy and workers' management of the major industries.

This socialist republic that was the ISRP's ideal required not just the overthrow of the economic system but also the ending of British domination in Ireland. The call for the ending of British rule marks a significant difference between the ISRP's programme and those of the British ILP or SDF. Both British socialist organisations supported some form of Home Rule rather than outright independence for Ireland.

Although state ownership of industry was one of the central aims of the ISRP, it is clear that Connolly did not view state ownership as sufficient in itself to constitute a socialist society. Rather, workers' ownership and control over industry were to be the main barometer test of how healthy a socialist society was. Indeed, Connolly pointed out that many liberal politicians of the period, who could not have been described as socialist, were in favour of some nationalisation in the economy:

> Socialism properly implies above all things the co-operative control by the workers of the machinery of production; without this co-operative control the public ownership by the State is not Socialism – it is only State capitalism . . . Therefore, we repeat, state ownership and control is not necessarily Socialism – if it were, then the Army, the Navy, the Police, the Judges, the Gaolers, the Informers, and the Hangmen, all would all be Socialist functionaries, as they are State officials – but the ownership by the State of all the land and materials for labour, combined with the co-operative control by the workers of such land and materials, would be Socialism.[61]

Democracy and workers' control through elections at the shop-floor level seem to form the heartbeat of the ISRP's vision of the eventual Irish Socialist Republic. Whether state control of industry in itself constituted a socialist economy was to become a much bigger issue within the socialist movement forty years after this programme was finalised by the ISRP. The existence of a state-controlled economy in the Soviet Union led many on the political right, as well as some on the left, to believe that socialism could exist in a society that was clearly undemocratic. Speculating how a political party would have reacted to a historical situation that occured many years after its own demise is always a task fraught with many difficulties. Yet it can be clearly seen from the programme of the ISRP that democracy was essential to the socialist society that the party wanted to found. A state-controlled economy in itself was not sufficient to make the relations of production socialist.

While it is true to say that Connolly and the ISRP would not have supported the Stalinist Soviet state, it can be said with equal certainty that they would not have viewed modern social democracy as socialism either. Proinsias Mac Aonghusa has written that 'Aspects of socialism evolved democratically in Scandinavian countries, and the sort of society envisaged by James Connolly became a reality in Norway, Sweden, and Denmark.'[62] This is simply untrue. The political programme of the ISRP looks to the establishment of a socialist society that would see the means of production controlled collectively through the auspicies of a democratically elected state. There would no longer be a capitalist class in the republic envisioned by the ISRP: it would be workers who would control society. This radical vision of a workers' democracy is a far cry from the admittedly social democratic but nonetheless capitalist countries that have evolved in the Scandinavian countries since the Second World War. While there is a large state and a developed social welfare system in each of these countries, there remains a capitalist class and private capital remains a hugely significant economic player. In the years following the collapse of the ISRP Connolly may have changed his views on how to achieve socialism, but his general view on how a socialist society would function adhered very much to what the ISRP wrote on the subject. It would be a society completely free from capitalism and run democratically by the proletariat.

Another ISRP member, Edward Stewart, described in August 1898 whom the Irish working class would have to get rid of before a socialist society became possible:

> Remember this, the Government-managed industries at the present time are merely a form of capitalism. We will not have arrived at Socialism till we have laid the foundation of a social system, in

which we shall have rid ourselves of the idlers, who live by taxing the community in the shape of rent, interest, and profit.[63]

So it was not only the British army and the British machinery of state that had to be defeated by the ISRP and the working class, but also the capitalist and landowners, both Irish and British, who controlled the levers of economic power in Ireland:

> By the use of the revolutionary ballot we will have made the very air of Ireland as laden with 'treason', as fully charged with the spirit of revolt, as it is to-day with the cant of compromise and the mortal sin of flunkeyism; and thus we will have laid a substantial groundwork for more effective action in the future, while to those whom we must remove in our onward march the pledge of our faith in the Social Revolution will convey the assurance that if we crush their profit-making enterprise to-day, yet when the sun dawns upon our freedom, if they have served their fellow creatures loyally in the hour of strife, they and their children and their children's children will be guaranteed against want and privation for all time by the safest guarantee man ever received, the guarantee backed by all the gratitude, the loyal hearts, the brains and industry of the Irish people, under the Irish Socialist Republic.[64]

While the objective of the ISRP, a socialist republic, was the final political goal for the party, the party also set out more modest demands in its programme, demands that it contended could be introduced under the contemporary capitalist system to alleviate the problems faced by the Irish working class. As part of the programme the ISRP made a short list of ten measures that it believed would help in 'restricting the tide of emigration by providing employment at home, and finally of palliating the evils of our present social system'. The ten-point programme would not be an end in itself, but would help to improve the lot of the working class under capitalism. In a sense these reforms would not be economically sufficient in themselves to constitute a socialist republic, but would be 'minimum' demands that the party would work towards under the capitalist economic system. Of course the maximum demand of the 'Irish Socialist Republic' would need nothing less than the political and economic defeat of capitalism in Ireland, far beyond this ten-point plan.

The measures included in the programme are fairly consistent with similar demands made by other socialist parties in Europe at the time. Points one and seven deal with the familiar demand for nationalisation of the commanding heights of the economy. The railways and canals were to be the first to be nationalised, with a general aspiration to push for the 'gradual extension of the principle of public ownership and supply to all the necessaries of life'. The rudimentary elements of what would now be recognized as a national social welfare system were also called for.

Point nine calls for free education up to the highest level at university and number six aspires to the free maintenance of all children. This was to be paid for by a 'graduated income tax on all incomes over £400 per annum in order to provide funds for pensions to the aged, infirm and widows and orphans' – point four of the minimum programme. The ISRP also wanted to see the abolition of private banks and money-lending institutions, and the establishment of a state bank. This bank would be run by an elected board, thus reflecting the ISRP wish to democratise the economy and allow the working class as much say as possible in the financial affairs of the country.

In the realm of labour, the party made the need for 'legislative restriction of hours of labour to 48 per week and establishment of a minimum wage' point five of its programme. The demand for universal suffrage is point ten.

Point three and point eight dealt with specifically Irish issues. Point three was introduced because the ISRP believed that Irish agriculture needed all the help that it could get to modernise: thus it called for the pooling of the best machinery to help in that process of development. The measure looked to the establishment of rural depots to hold the most improved agricultural machinery. These depots would be state-run and would also be places where the best farming equipment could be lent out to the agricultural population at a rent covering cost and management alone. Point eight, in an attempt to break the religious hold over education in the schools in Ireland, looks to 'public control and management of National schools by boards elected by popular ballot for that purpose alone'.

These measures relating to agriculture and religious teachings in schools were raised specifically in an Irish context. Combined with the references in the wider programme to the subjection of Ireland by Britain, the programme contained much that was particular to the Irish political context. The references to the Irish situation reflect the adaptability of the ISRP's document, which, although it was inspired by the other European socialist parties' programmes, did not stick rigidly to any standard text. The need to take into account 'national' factors when composing a socialist programme was to become a major issue within the Second International in the decades after 1896. In 1914, when writing on the need for socialists to defend the right of self-determination for colonised nations, Lenin wrote that there could be no question of the Marxists of any country drawing up their national programme without taking into account all the general historical and concrete state conditions of the particular country in question. He believed that socialists should defend the right of nations to self-determination as a matter of principle: 'Bourgeois nationalism of any oppressed nation has a general democratic content that is directed against oppression and it is this content that we unconditionally support.'[65] The ISRP was one of the first socialist organisations in any colonised nation to put the need for self-determination at the heart of its political programme.

The final section of the programme was quite succinct in describing which way the ISRP believed to be the most effective in attempting to achieve socialism. Social reforms were to be pursued by fighting elections and attempting to get ISRP members elected into public office. The ISRP stressed the need for electoral work, although it made it clear that changes that could be brought through the ballot box were not going to be enough in themselves to sound the death knell for capitalism or herald the onset of socialism. It is clear that at this stage Connolly and the ISRP were in a classic social-democratic period. They believed that the best way of achieving socialism was by winning control of the elected bodies that were open to socialists to contest. However, this stance was a tactical one and by the time of the Boer War Connolly was already openly contemplating, if the political conditions had been favourable, an armed uprising as a way of advancing leftist politics. The very fact that the ISRP's members threw themselves into street politics shows that the party did not believe that the only way to highlight and propagate socialist politics was by standing in elections. The programme contained no 'insurrectionary notions', as Morgan argues:

> Working-class advance would be by electoral means, but there was a hint of the need for revolutionary class struggle on the eve of power.[66]

Demonstrations, public meetings and written propaganda were all parts of the general party work, but elections were of central importance for the organisation. When the party made its decision to stand a candidate in the local elections in January 1899 it made it

quite clear that any reforms that an elected socialist could introduce
would of necessity be limited:

> The Socialist Republican Party, whilst keeping steadily before its
> members and sympathisers the necessity for broader and more
> sweeping changes than any municipality can effect, has yet never
> lost sight of the needs of the moment or ignored the immediate
> practical measures which must be enforced in the interest of the
> workers.[67]

After stating its ultimate goal and its list of ten minimum demands
under the present system, the programme gives a clear justification
for the party's beliefs, and why it believed socialism was ultimately a
just and honest cause for which to strive:

> That the agricultural and industrial system of a free people, like
> their political system, ought to be an accurate reflex of the
> democratic principle by the people for the people, solely in the
> interests of the people. That the private ownership, by a class, of the
> land and instruments of production, distribution and exchange, is
> opposed to this vital principle of justice, and is the fundamental
> basis of all oppression, national, political and social. That the
> subjection of one nation to another, as of Ireland to the authority of
> the British Crown, is a barrier to the free political and economic
> development of the subjected nation, and can only serve the
> interests of the exploiting classes of both nations. That, therefore,
> the national and economic freedom of the Irish people must be
> sought in the same direction, viz., the establishment of an Irish
> Socialist Republic, and the consequent conversion of the means of
> production, distribution and exchange into the common property of
> society, to be held and controlled by a democratic state in the
> interests of the entire community. That the conquest by the Social
> Democracy of political power in Parliament, and on all public
> bodies in Ireland, is the readiest and most effective means whereby
> the revolutionary forces may be organised and disciplined to attain
> that end.[68]

A number of historians have commented on how 'orthodox', in terms
of the general layout, the programme is. The programme very much
follows the Second International view that socialist parties should
have both 'minimum' and 'maximum' demands. The stress laid on
the need for the socialist parties to fight initially for socialism through
the ballot box, rather than any form of insurrection or mass
revolution, was also common across the parties of the Second
International. The influence that the general programme of the British

SDF had on the ISRP's programme must also be highlighted. Connolly had been very impressed with the SDF in the early years of his political development. Henry Hyndman, the leading figure in the SDF, wrote a pamphlet called *Socialism Made Plain* that particularly influenced the ISRP's programme. The SDF, Connolly believed at the time, represented the most radical edge of the British labour movement and he used much of their general philosophy to guide the drafting of the ISRP's programme. However, as will be discussed later (in Chapter Four), it was the inclusion of the demand for national liberation for Ireland from Britain that was the most original element of the ISRP's programme. This demand would lead to some friction between the two organisations in future years. A socialist party in a colonised country calling on the proletariat of that country to actively campaign for a socialist society, while also fighting for an independent nation, was almost unheard of in the international socialist movement. The programme also stood in the general historical tradition of the *Communist Manifesto* written by Marx and Engels. The *Manifesto* included a list of ten minimum demands that Marx and Engels claimed Communists should make part of their general propaganda.

In theory at least the programme remained the central plank describing the aims and objectives of the party. As we have seen, it remained unaltered for the eight years of the existence of the ISRP and was always displayed prominently in the written propaganda of the party. It served as the theoretical bedrock from which the party could begin its period of active socialist campaigning, with the anti-Jubilee mobilisation in 1897 and the political activity centred around the 1798 centenary commemorations that were held the following year.

THE 1798 COMMEMORATION AND THE ANTI-JUBILEE PROTEST

In June 1897 Dublin was being prepared for the upcoming celebrations of Queen Victoria's Diamond Jubilee. The ISRP was the main instigator behind the major mobilisation in opposition to the official celebrations of Victoria's sixty years on the throne. Side by side with Maud Gonne, the ISRP launched a very active campaign, highlighting the wrongs overseen by the Empire in Ireland since the time of the Great Famine, which occurred during the very early years of Victoria's reign.

Connolly sought to involve the 1798 Committees and the republicans in the anti-Jubilee protest. The committees had been formed in early 1897 to organise the centenary celebrations of the 1798 rebellion that were to be held the following year. The 1798 rebellion had been led by the Protestant republican Wolfe Tone and inspired by the French Revolution. The French government had given military aid to the rebellion, but, despite some major battles, the British had defeated the rebels. The rebellion had also briefly united both Catholic and Protestant against British rule over the island.

In the beginning the 1798 Committees were run by radical republicans and socialists, while the more conservative Home Rule politicians remained aloof. Despite this, the committees refused to organise a mass demonstration against the British Empire during the Jubilee festivities and instead decided to hold a Convention on the day of Victoria's visit to Ireland. The ISRP ignored this and went ahead with its very own major protest, which was given practical support by that idiosyncratic doyenne of Irish republicanism, Maud Gonne. On the eve of Jubilee Day, 21 June 1897, the ISRP's protest and meeting took place on College Green, with a large crowd in attendance. A number of Jubilee-supporting Trinity College students attacked the protest, but were repelled by the ISRP members, who overpowered their attackers. On the day of the Jubilee itself the ISRP marched through the centre of Dublin with a symbolic coffin, representing the Irish deaths during the Great Famine:

> It proved to be popular. There was a parade around Dublin with these banners and they carried a coffin painted black, and on each side in very large white letters were the words 'the British Empire' after that was paraded around the city it was launched into the Liffey at O'Connell Bridge, to thunderous applause from the people who marched.[69]

Riots followed this incident and police baton-charged the crowds of Dubliners who had decided to turn to smashing any business premises displaying any pro-Jubilee presentations. The police attacked the ISRP's offices and the Crown forces went on to physically attack individual members of the party.

As we have seen, in 1897 the party took a favourable view of the newly formed 1798 Committees. At the party's meeting on 21 January 1897 the ISRP decided to join in the celebration of the 1798 rebellion and it was agreed that the ISRP would write to the Young Ireland Society applying for permission to send delegates to the committee.

For Connolly and the ISRP the 1798 Commemorations clearly showed the political gap between Wolfe Tone and the other leaders of the 1798 Rebellion, and the politics of the Home Rule Party of their own day. While trying desperately to hold on to some sort of mantle as heirs to Wolfe Tone's vision, the Home Rulers were, in Connolly's opinion, the absolute polar opposite of everything that Wolfe Tone had stood for. Connolly mercilessly criticised the Home Rulers as nothing more than conservative and reactionary upholders of the economic and political status quo. For Connolly Wolfe Tone and the other rebels represented the high point of revolutionary practice by Irish republicans. While the Home Rulers on the surface celebrated the 1798 rebellion, the ISRP believed that they wanted nothing to do with the revolutionary ideology espoused by the rebels of 1798, in fact the Home Rule Party feared a rebellion, particularly on the part of the Irish working class in the Ireland of 1897–98:

> The mixed character of all speeches in connection with the '98 movement, at the banquet and elsewhere, proves conclusively that our middle-class leaders are afraid to trust democracy. In the midst of their most fervent vituperations against the British Government, there rises up before their mind's eye the spectacle of the Irish working people demanding Freedom for their class from the economic slavery of to-day. And struck with affright [*sic*] the middle-class politician buttons up his trousers pocket, and shoving his hand deep into the pockets of his working class compatriots, cries out as his fingers close upon the plunder: 'No class questions in Irish politics.'[70]

By 1898 the *Workers' Republic* was filled with Connolly's polemical outbursts against the Home Rulers, who had by this stage decided to become more involved in the 1798 Commemorations and had begun to join the 1798 Committees. Connolly believed that the Home Rulers were now attempting to use the committee and the celebrations of the rebellion to help to bolster their own disunited political organisation. As usual, it was from the pen of Connolly, that the Home Rulers were attacked, this time in verse:

> NATIONAL ANTHEM
> (For the use of Home Rule Editors)
> Who fears to speak of '98,
> Who blushes at the name,
> God save our Gracious Queen,

Long may she reign.
He's all a knave or half a slave
Who slights his country thus,
But we Home Rule men can fool men
Who put their trust in us.
(Refrain)
Send her victorious, happy and glorious,
Long to reign over us,
God save the Queen.[71]

As 1898 progressed and the centenary celebrations came into view, it became clear to the ISRP that the 1798 Committees had been colonised by the conservative Home Rule Party. The ISRP formed its own '98 Rank and File group, and argued against any further involvement by the Home Rulers in the centenary celebrations. However, its protestations fell on deaf ears and in the end the commemoration was marked by a conservative march through the centre of Dublin that had representatives from the Catholic capitalist class, principally in the persons of William Martin Murphy, the Ancient Order of Hibernians and various Home Rule politicians on the platform. The Home Rule Party had become involved in the event late in the day and used it as a springboard to help to heal the wounds created by the Parnell split in the early 1890s.

Writing one year later, this time about how the republicans had allowed the Home Rulers onto a pro-Boer platform, Connolly again attacked the advanced nationalists for allowing the Home Rulers to make political capital from protests that they had little real sympathy for: 'The Nationalist anti-war meeting was a major success – for the Home Rulers. It has resuscitated their party in the minds of the people and taught them to look to Home Rule politicians for light and leading.'[72]

The '98 Rank and File group formed by the ISRP was really little more than a front organisation for the party. It had few members who were not already members of the ISRP and its meetings took place just before the ISRP's weekly meeting, the attendees at each being almost exactly the same.

In article after article in the *Workers' Republic* the ISRP argued that the spirit of revolution shown by the rebels of 1798 had more in common with the politics of the ISRP than anything that the Home Rule Party stood for:

Wolfe Tone was abreast of the revolutionary thought of his day, as are the Socialist Republicans of our day. He saw clearly, as we see, that a dominion as long-rooted in any country as the British dominion in Ireland can only be dislodged by a revolutionary impulse in line with the development of the entire epoch. Grasping this truth in all its fullness he broke with the so-called 'practical' men of the time, and wherever he could get a hearing he, by voice and pen, inculcated the republican principles of the French Revolution and counselled his countrymen to embark the national movement on the crest of that revolutionary wave. His Irish birth did not create his hatred of the British Constitution, but only intensified it.[73]

For a brief period Connolly also attacked the republicans in the pages of the *Workers' Republic*, principally for their continued policy of sharing platforms with conservative, albeit 'nationalist', politicians. The republicans, the ISRP believed, shared an insanely broad platform with the Home Rule politicians: 'They will have no exclusiveness, they tell us, and open their ranks to all who like to enter, no questions asked.'[74]

However, this outburst of criticism of the republicans following the 1798 commemorations was fleeting, and it was not long before the party was again forging links with advanced nationalists on other issues. Connolly tried to build up a working relationship with Arthur Griffith in particular. Griffith was the editor of the *United Irishman* and was a printer by trade. He had spent time in South Africa as a young man and had returned to Ireland to become a political activist. He was in favour of an independent Ireland, of sorts, with a strong capitalist economy based on self-reliance. His paper was renamed *Sinn Féin* in 1906. In 1905 the party known as Sinn Féin was formed from an amalgamation of a number of republican groups (including the National Council, the Dungannon Clubs and Cumann na nGaedheal). It was with this republican milieu that Connolly and his party tried to engage politically throughout the lifetime of the ISRP.

NOTES

1. Christine Kinealy, *This Great Calamity: The Irish Famine 1845–52* (Dublin: Gill & Macmillan, 1994).
2. James Connolly, *Labour in Irish History* (London: Bookmarks, 1987), p. 136.
3. See Connolly, *Labour in Irish History*, p. 131.
4. Karl Marx and Frederick Engels, *Ireland and the Irish Question* (Moscow: Progress Publishers, 1971), p. 138.

5. P. Dubois, *Contemporary Ireland* (Dublin: Maunsell, 1908), p. 231.
6. Mary Daly, *Dublin the Deposed Capital: A Social and Economic History 1860–1914* (Cork: Cork University Press, 1984), p. 18.
7. Belinda Probert, *Beyond Orange and Green* (London: The Academy Press, 1978), p. 24.
8. Kieran Allen, *Is Ireland a Neo Colony?* (Dublin: Bookmarks, 1990), p. 11.
9. See Marx and Engels, *Ireland and the Irish Question*.
10. Ibid., p. 132.
11. Ibid., pp. 161–2.
12. Chris Bambery, *Ireland's Permanent Revolution* (London: Bookmarks, 1990), pp. 29–30.
13. Marx and Engels, *Ireland*, p. 162.
14. Daly, *Dublin the Deposed Capital*, p. 50.
15. Fintan Lane, *The Origins of Modern Irish Socialism, 1881–1896* (Cork: Cork University Press, 1997).
16. Ibid., p. 203.
17. *Justice*, 14 Dec. 1895.
18. Helen Clarke, *Sing a Rebel Song: The Story of James Connolly* (Edinburgh: City of Edinburgh District Council and Irish History Workshop, 1989), p. 8.
19. Desmond Greaves, *The Life and Times of Connolly* (London: Lawrence & Wishart, 1971), p. 53.
20. For more details regarding Connolly's early political life in Edinburgh see Greaves, *The Life and Times*, pp. 11–72. Kieran Allen, *The Politics of James Connolly* (London: Pluto Press, 1990), pp. 1–13.
21. According to Thomas Lyng, there were eight men at the first meeting and he took their names: Sean Cronin, *Young Connolly* (Dublin: Repsol, 1983), p. 30. Connolly wrote of six men when reminiscing about the origins of the party in 1902. Lyng's account seems the more reliable.
22. Minutes, 29 May 1896, in Minutes of the Irish Socialist Republican Party, 1898–1904, MS 16264–67, O'Brien Collection, National Library of Ireland (NLI).
23. *Workers' Republic* (WR), Vol. 1, No. 11, 22 October 1898.
24. The pen-pictures of the ISRP members are compiled from a variety of sources: Minutes of the ISRP, 1896–97 MS 13593, O'Brien Collection NLI, Minutes of the Irish Socialist Republican Party, 1898–1904, MS 16264–67, O'Brien Collection, NLI, 'The Early Propagandists of the ISRP Party', MS 15704(i), O'Brien Collection, NLI, William O'Brien, *Forth the Banners Go* (Dublin: Three Candles, 1969), Cronin, *Young Connolly*.
25. Minutes, 17 June 1897, in Minutes of the ISRP, 1896–97, MS 13593, O'Brien Collection NLI.
26. Lane, *The Origins of Modern Irish Socialism*, p. 219.
27. Minutes, 3 Oct. 1898.
28. O'Brien, *Forth the Banners Go*, p. 5.
29. Clarke, *Sing a Rebel Song*, p. 11, Greaves, *Life and Times*, p. 59.
30. Austen Morgan, *Political Biography of James Connolly* (Manchester: Manchester University Press, 1988), p. 28.
31. Priscilla Metscher, *James Connolly and the Reconquest of Ireland* (Minnesota,

Marxist Educational Press/Nature, Society and Thought, 2002), p. 27.

32. *WR*, Vol. 2, No. 8, 15 July 1899.
33. Minutes, 4 Dec. 1898.
34. Minutes, 30 Jan. 1899.
35. Cronin, *Young Connolly*, p. 34.
36. As cited in Minutes, various dates.
37. Minutes, 6 July 1903.
38. Cronin, *Young Connolly*, p. 67.
39. Dan O'Brien, *Public Health and Capitalism: Being the Report of a Lecture Delivered before the Dublin Branch of the Irish Socialist Republican Party* (Dublin: *Workers' Republic* Pamphlet, no date), LO P70 (NLI).
40. *WR*, Vol. 4, No. 33, March 1902.
41. Minutes, 13 March 1899.
42. Cronin, *Young Connolly*, p. 58.
43. *WR*, Vol. 2, No. 28, 30 Dec. 1899.
44. Sean O' Casey, *Autobiographies 1* (New York: Carroll & Graf, 1984), p. 414. While O'Casey's general reminiscence of the public meeting is probably correct, it is impossible that James Connolly's pamphlet *Socialism Made Easy* was being sold to the crowd. That pamphlet was not published until Connolly was in America (1908), four years after the fall of the ISRP.
45. *WR*, Vol. 1, No. 8, 27 Aug. 1898.
46. *WR*, Vol. 1, No. 5, 10 Sept. 1898.
47. Cronin, *Young Connolly*, pp. 59–67.
48. Connolly, 'Introduction' *Erin's Hope* (New York: 1909) (publisher unknown)
49. *WR*, Vol. 2, No. 20, 21 Oct. 1899.
50. *WR*, Vol. 4, No. 30, Oct. 1901.
51. See Frank Callaghan, *The Appeal to the Hillsides: Parnell and the Fenians, 1890–91* in Donal McCartney, *Parnell: The Politics of Power* (Dublin: Wolfhound Press, 1991).
52. *WR*, Vol. 1, No. 9, 8 Oct. 1898.
53. Minutes, 7 Jan. 1897.
54. O'Brien, *Forth the Banners Go*, p. 14.
55. Minutes, 8 Oct. 1896.
56. *WR*, Vol. 2, No. 19, 7 Oct. 1899.
57. Minutes, 10 April 1899.
58. Minutes, 13 March 1899.
59. Cronin, *Young Connolly*, p. 33.
60. The programme is also reproduced in full in Appendix One of this book.
61. Connolly, *The New Evangel* (1905), in *Erin's Hope, The End and the Means* (Dublin and Belfast: New Books Publications, 1972), p. 27.
62. Proinsias Mac Aonghusa, *What Connolly Said* (Dublin: New Island Books, 1995), p. 10.
63. *WR*, Vol. 1, No. 3, 27 Aug. 1898.
64. Connolly, *Erin's Hope*, p. 23.
65. V.I. Lenin, *The Right of Nations to Self-Determination* (Moscow: Progress Publishers, 1968), p. 54.
66. Morgan, *Political Biography*, p. 26.

67. *WR*, Vol. 1, No. 11, 22 Oct. 1898.
68. See Appendix One.
69. O'Brien, *Forth the Banners Go*, p. 9.
70. *WR*, Vol. 1, No. 2, 20 Aug. 1898.
71. Ibid.
72. *WR*, Vol. 2, No. 23, 18 Nov. 1899.
73. Cronin, *Young Connolly*, p. 50.
74. *WR*, Vol. 1, No. 4, 3 Sept. 1898.

CHAPTER TWO

The Class Struggle in Practice, 1898–1900

The establishment of a leftist paper to propagate the views of the ISRP and disseminate socialist ideas within the Irish working class was always one of Connolly's primary aims. The ISRP was in existence two years before it finally founded its own paper, but it had gained some publication experience from producing leaflets and pamphlets during this period. The *Workers' Republic*, which was first published in August 1898, was to have an often difficult and irregular history. However, it served its purpose of highlighting a socialist viewpoint within the general political milieu of Ireland at the turn of the century, as well as serving as a ready-made literary mouthpiece for Connolly to express his politics.[1] It was also a landmark publication in the history of left-wing journalism in Ireland. While there had been a number of other radical papers produced by 'advanced nationalists' during the nineteenth century, the *Workers' Republic* was the first paper to fuse both radical commentary on the news of the day, including both national and international coverage, with longer, more discursive pieces dealing with the finer points of socialist philosophy.

The paper included an impressive array of international labour news, reflecting the deep internationalist perspective of the ISRP. Articles were reprinted from a vast number of international leftist journals, thus giving evidence of Connolly's wide reading while working as editor of the paper. The *Workers' Call* of Chicago, the *Brisbane Worker* and the San Francisco *Examiner* were particular favourites, articles from which appeared in the pages of the *Workers' Republic* with some regularity.

The *Workers' Republic* commenced publication on 13 August 1898, initially as a weekly. The paper ceased temporarily on 22 October 1898, but was recommenced on 12 May 1899 and then appeared somewhat irregularly until 10 February 1901, when it ceased publication again until 12 May 1900. It became a fortnightly from 27 October 1900 and a monthly from February 1901, and appeared even less frequently until it ceased publication entirely, shortly before Connolly's departure to the United States in May 1903. The paper's original articles were nearly all written in the ISRP's offices at 67 Middle Abbey Street. Graham and Co. Printers on Ryder's Row in Dublin printed the early issues of the paper.

The first issue was dated on 13 August 1898, cost one penny and was eight pages long. It already carried many of the features that were to grace its pages until 1903. The foundation of the new paper was advertised in *Justice*, the paper of the British Social Democratic Federation (SDF), the publication in which Connolly had advertised his 'services' as a socialist organiser just three years before. The *Workers' Republic* was partially funded with a loan from the leader of the British Independent Labour Party (ILP), James Keir Hardie. Hardie gave the party a £50 loan, a substantial sum in 1898, to be repaid at £10 a month. In the end only one payment was made, something that must have stung Keir Hardie a little more a few years later when he was on the receiving end of some fierce criticism from the ISRP regarding his open support for the Home Rule Party.[2]

The front-page article 'Home Thrust', written by Connolly under the pseudonym 'Spailpin' (which means 'immigrant labourer' in Gaelic), was generally a mixture of witty left-wing observations on the issues of the day. Other ISRP members also used *noms-de plume* when writing in the pages of the paper. Edward Stewart signed his articles 'Yumen', while Con O'Lyhane went under the name of 'Proletarian', John Arnall used 'Kernuak' and Connolly himself also sometimes used 'Setanta'.

In his first-ever 'Home Thrust' column Connolly warned the politicians of rival political organisations what they could expect from his pen. The first issue of the paper carried this sharp warning to the opponents of socialism in Ireland: 'The large number of time-servers, wire-pullers, and notoriety hunters in the Irish movement here, may only expect to receive sharp and unmerciful criticism.'[3] The first issue also contained an article by party member Edward Stewart dealing with the situation among tramway workers in Dublin in relation to pay and working conditions.

There were also various short reports from across the worldwide labour movement, which were gathered in regular columns entitled 'World Siftings' and 'Continental Jottings'. These two columns mainly consisted of small snippets of information taken from various leftist papers and journals, including (besides those mentioned above) *La Petite Republique* (France), *Il Proletario* (Italy), *The Vorwärts* (Germany), and the *Labour Leader* (Great Britain).

The paper often included four-page supplements, mainly transcribing lectures given by ISRP members at public meetings or as in the *Workers' Republic* in December 1900, 'A Novel Christmas Sermon *Presenting A Parable*' written by an English Socialist – a satire upon the Christianity of the English State Church.[4]

The 'Home Thrusts' column quickly became a favourite among the *Workers' Republic*'s readership with a number of witty asides and satirical takes on some homespun rhetoric, such as the following: "Father", said the little boy, "why do the story books always speak of their heroes as being born of poor but honest parents why don't they ever say rich but honest parents." "Because my child, if they did nobody would believe them."'[5]

It was the Home Rule Party and its politicians who were the principal targets of Spailpin's considerable caustic wit:

> Nothing impresses the reader so much as what he does not understand. That is why we have so long admired the Home Rule leaders. They but needed to open their mouths and talk, and talk, and talk and still to talk, and the more they talked the less that we understood and consequently the more we admired them. We just stood around with our mouths open like a Malahide codfish, waiting for the tide to come in.[6]

The front page declared that the *Workers' Republic* was to be a 'Literary Champion of the Irish Democracy', and that the paper advocated an Irish Republic, abolition of landlordism and wage slavery, and the establishment of co-operative organisation of labour under Irish representative governing bodies. Every issue of the paper from 1898 until 1903 carried a full copy of the ISRP's programme, and the front page also displayed the party's harp and shamrock insignia. The first volume of the *Workers' Republic*, which ran until 22 October 1898, was almost entirely written by Connolly himself, although Stewart contributed a number of articles and the international stories were lifted, as mentioned, from other left-leaning papers.

Connolly also published a series of articles in the *Workers' Republic* that were eventually compiled to form his most famous book, *Labour in Irish History*.[7] This contains Connolly's principal written analysis of the history of the Irish working class, and its fight against British imperialism and capitalism. Although the series was not published in book form until 1910, its sixteen chapters had all appeared in the *Workers' Republic* by 1903.

Plagued by a chronic lack of finance, the *Workers' Republic* had a turbulent first few months and the decision taken by the party in late 1898, that what funds it had available should go towards fighting the upcoming local elections, led to the suspension of the paper. The party always had problems with its internal finance. In November 1898 it passed a motion censuring the Secretary and auditors for not producing a corrected audit for the party. This problem was to continue to plague the organisation and was to occupy the minds of party members throughout the five years in which the paper appeared.

The party accepted some advertisements in an attempt to try and raise money. Notices for Neary's Bar in Grafton Street, and for M.J. Lord's Bicycle Shop, Wynn Street, Birmingham, show that the paper was seeking, and probably finding readers outside the island of Ireland and among the drinkers of Dublin. A single insertion in the paper of an advertisement cost two shillings and six pence per inch, while a standing advertisement could be negotiated at a special price. Trade union advertisements in the paper were free, as long as the notice was less than 20 words in length. A list of wholesalers selling the *Workers' Republic* gives an idea of the wide range of geographical sources from which readers could purchase the official organ of the ISRP: Dublin (Eason & Son), Cork, Drogheda, Limerick, Belfast, Liverpool, London, Glasgow, Dundee, Edinburgh, Manchester.

The paper could also be bought in the United States, from members of the Socialist Labour Party (SLP).[8] The SLP, a radical socialist party, stood well to the left of the more reformist Social Democrat organisation.

With these wide-ranging points of distribution it is very difficult to get a sense of the actual number of sales achieved by the *Workers' Republic*, although we can safely say that the paper was a lot more successful than the party itself in reaching out to a wider public. Although poverty and illiteracy in Dublin greatly reduced the potential readership of the paper, the *Workers' Republic* does seem to have had an impact on the general milieu involved in the Irish cultural revival. Certain sectors of Dublin's workers, such as the dockers for a brief period, also seem to have bought the paper in substantial numbers. Whenever the party focused on any set of workers, as it did with the dockers during their strike in 1900, party members set out to sell the paper to the most militant and politically conscious individuals in specific workplaces. The paper was also sold at public meetings and large political protests, such as the 1798 centenary commemorations, the anti-Boer War marches in 1899 and the commemoration for the Manchester Martyrs held in Dublin in 1900.

The party got some idea of the surprising background of some of the paper's readership in the Dublin business community in rather unfortunate circumstances in June 1900. A Dublin businessman with nationalist leanings, John McGuinness, served a writ for criminal libel on the *Workers' Republic* after an article appeared in the paper regarding McGuinness and his behaviour during a bitter tailors' strike in the capital city. The *Workers' Republic* essentially said that McGuinness (who had become known as a minor poet writing lyrics in praise of the Boer armies fighting against the British during the Boer War) had been blacklegging the Dublin tailors in an attempt to break their strike. The *Workers' Republic* had cheerfully named McGuinness the 'poet laureate of sweating'.[9] McGuinness was infuriated, not least after copies of the *Workers' Republic* had been posted up on trees and walls in the west Dublin town of Lucan, with the article in question underlined. According to McGuinness, his fellow businessmen, who, intriguingly, seemed to be avid readers of the *Workers' Republic*, had read the article and his name had been blackened by the contents of the piece.

> The said article is a false and malicious libel on me and calculated to provide a breach of the peace by inciting the Tailors on strike and their sympathisers to molest me and my employees and it has already caused me serious injury in my business. [The *Workers' Republic*] is much read by persons with whom I have business relations and with whom my said business brings me in contact.[10]

The case petered out in the end, although Connolly mounted a robust defence of the paper at the original court hearing. While cross-examining McGuinness, Connolly was able to make the employer admit under oath that he used non-union labour and that many of the men he employed could have been blacklegs. The judge immediately threw the case out of court after this admission.

The paper also got into a dispute with a well-known nationalist journalist of the time, Fred Allen, over an article that stated that he had stood for the playing of 'God Save the Queen' during an annual dinner of Dublin's journalists.

The Land League leader Michael Davitt was an early subscriber and supporter of the paper. Letters from members of the American SLP welcoming the publication of the paper were also printed. Despite the interest that the paper was receiving, it was still proving difficult to find the money to print it and, as we have seen, the first volume came to an abrupt halt before the end of 1898. A second volume began the following May and ran until February 1900. The first issue of the second volume began by bravely contending that the future of the paper now seemed bright:

> We have now a paper of our own, a printing plant of our own, and a staff as capable of giving a reasoned exposition of the faith that is in them as any in Ireland. We are therefore free of that dependence on the goodwill of a capitalist printer which cramped our efforts in the past.[11]

While references to a 'staff' of writers around the *Workers' Republic* were highly optimistic, there had been an increase in the number of party members contributing to the paper's editorial content. Con O'Lyhane, the founder of the party's Cork branch, started a column under the pseudonym 'Proletarian': his 'Notes from the Rebel City' described how the party was faring in Cork, the largest city on the south coast. Further articles from Stewart and Murtagh Lyng (who was to become the editor of the paper when Connolly was abroad on speaking tours) were also printed in the paper. Old articles by John Mitchell and even lyrics by the great romantic poet Shelley were printed in the pages of the *Workers' Republic*.

Getting the paper published was always a struggle, with few party members having the ability to contribute in any meaningful sense. It is a reflection of the commitment, resourcefulness and hard work of Connolly in particular that such a small organisation was able to publish any sort of paper for any length of time. As if to anger the overworked Connolly even further, there was growing disquiet among members of the Dublin Typographical Association, who complained that 'blacklegs' were producing the *Workers' Republic* as it was being put together by the voluntary labour of party members. Connolly met the association and made his own views clear, arguing: 'When we shave, do we blackleg on barbers?'

The paper was heavily reliant on the hard labour provided by Connolly himself. During a period in August 1900 when Connolly was too ill to edit the paper, it was simply not produced. Yet, despite all the effort and persistent hard work put in by the ISRP's volunteers, it was almost inevitable, given the circumstances, that deadlines were missed and subscriptions not fulfilled. Connolly wrote to the paper's subscribers in August of 1899 and told them honestly about the problems faced by the paper:

> For the information of subscribers, who may feel inclined to grumble at a little irregularity in the delivery of our paper, we would again remind our readers that the whole work of producing this journal is performed by the voluntary labour of the members of the Dublin branch of the Irish Socialist Republican Party.[12]

In later years Thomas Lyng outlined the sacrifice made by comrades in getting the paper published, but, even while he was praising the work of the many, he could not but recognise the almost superhuman effort made by Connolly:

> Many of our members, after toiling for a capitalist during the day, had to spend the entire evening in [the] arduous work of a printing press and Mr Connolly had to be for years at one and the same the editor, compositor, assistant printer, principal writer, speaker, and organiser.[13]

Connolly saw the paper as essential to any political success the ISRP might have. The *Workers' Republic* was to serve as the eyes and ears of the party, carrying reports on events organised by the ISRP, providing socialist commentary on the issues of the day, discussing issues ignored by the mainstream capitalist press and helping to forge links with the membership of the party across the country. The *Workers' Republic* encouraged debate and discussions, and invited readers to write letters asking questions about the fundamental points of socialism. If the paper received any letters, they were always displayed prominently and Connolly – for it was nearly always him – would provide full and detailed answers to readers' enquiries.

The *Workers' Republic* under Connolly's editorship did not fall into the trap of many left-wing papers, by becoming nothing more than the literary battleground for ideological warfare between various left-wing groups. Rather, the paper kept out of the skirmishes between socialist organisations:

As a general rule we refrain from taking notice in our columns of the quarrels or discussions of the Socialist parties of the world. We regard ourselves as being, at present, primarily a missionary organ, founded for the purpose of presenting to the working class of Ireland a truer and more scientific understanding of the principles of Socialism than they could derive from a perusal of the scant and misleading references to that subject to be found in the ordinary capitalist press. This task also involves, as a matter of course, the criticism and exposure of all the quack remedies and political trickeries with which our masters, or their ignorant imitators in the ranks of the workers themselves, seek to impose upon the people as cure-alls for our social evils. We have all along acted upon the conviction that we must give the revolutionary principles of Socialism an Irish home and habitation before we venture to express our opinions on the minor matters dividing the party abroad.[14]

The paper generally looked outwards and took on the political enemies on the right rather than participating in the squabbles of the left. In some ways it is interesting to compare Connolly's concept of the socialist newspaper with that of the Russian socialist Vladimir Illyich Lenin, who gave the subject some thought, almost contemporaneously with Connolly's time as editor of the *Workers' Republic*, in his work *What is to be Done* (1902).[15] Drawing on his experience on the editorial board of the Russian socialist paper *Iskra*, Lenin wrote about the organisational role that a paper should play in the workings of a socialist party.

A newspaper is not only a collective propagandist and a collective agitator, it is also a collective organiser. In this last respect it may be likened to the scaffolding around a building under construction, which marks the contours of the structure and facilitates communication between the builders, enabling them to distribute the work and to view the common results achieved by their organised labour.[16]

While Connolly never got round to so clearly articulating his view of the role of the socialist paper within the party, his actions as editor of the *Workers' Republic* point to an approach similar to Lenin's.

Connolly was extremely disappointed when the paper finally came to an end in 1903. He believed that the paper could have been made to pay for itself and cover other expenses run up by the party in the course of its work. It was with hope in his heart that Connolly again wrote about changes in the structure of the *Workers' Republic* in July

1902, changes that he believed would lead to a better future, but this was not to be. Connolly remained very honest about the past problems with the party's literary organ:

> Since that time 1898 the *Workers' Republic* has gone down into the valley of financial humiliation; going down just as our circulation began to touch the point at which we could clear expenses.[17]

The final split in the party in mid-1903 reflected the importance that Connolly ascribed to the *Workers' Republic*, while some comrades within the party obviously did not hold this view. Whatever its overall impact on the wider political sphere in Ireland during the period 1898–1903, there can be little doubt that the pages of the *Workers' Republic* served Connolly well as a template on which he could compose and publish his political writings in a public format. Connolly and the ISRP were able to make instant public statements on the great issues of the period, using an outlet denied to them in the mainstream capitalist press. These major issues included the outbreak of hostilities in South Africa in 1899, but the first volume of the *Workers' Republic* found itself primarily dealing with issues closer to home, predominantly the formation of the Labour Electoral Association in November 1898.

THE ISRP AND THE WIDER IRISH LABOUR MOVEMENT

The formation of the Labour Electoral Association (LEA) in Dublin in 1898 hardly seems now like a major moment in the history of the Irish working-class movement. Yet in 1898, when the political left was a barren place, the ISRP welcomed the foundation of the LEA as reflecting an important step in the political progress of the Irish proletariat.

The LEA was formed by the Dublin Trades Council at a well-attended special labour conference held on 27 August 1898 in the Trades Hall on Capel Street.[18] The LEA was basically a political expression of the Dublin Trades Council, which formed a provisional committee to run the association. The provisional committee included members from all the major trades in the city. The LEA itself comprised well-known members of the trades council and left-leaning politicians who had once been closer to the Home Rule camp. The LEA had become a political possibility following the passage of the Local Government Act 1898, which had enlarged the franchise to include a section of working men. Although the LEA's political positions were well to the right of the ISRP's, the *Workers' Republic* marked the formation of the LEA with a generally favourable article by Connolly. He described the LEA's formation as 'perhaps the most important step yet taken by the organised workers in Ireland':

> We repeat that we hail with joy this action of the Dublin trade unions, [and] our candidates will joyfully co-operate with them, for if they do not become lackeys of the capitalist class, they must inevitably become allies of the Socialist Republicans. We do not, however, labour under the belief that delegates so chosen will be socialists, or consciously in favour of socialist principles. On the contrary, we are quite prepared to find each and every one of these representatives solemnly repudiating the taint of socialism. But we do believe, and not only believe but know that every workingman elected to the Municipal Council of Dublin, if he be true to his class when elected, will find that every step he takes in the Council in furtherance of the interests of his class, must of necessity take the form of an application of socialist principles.[19]

In October 1898 the *Workers' Republic* reported on a public meeting in Fosters Place at which Connolly and Tom Lyng addressed the issue of the LEA. Connolly spoke in praise of the LEA, but pointed out the differences between his own party and the new association:

> He was a Trade Unionist, but he was more than a Trade Unionist. The Trade Unionist, who was only a Trade Unionist, was to the socialist what the believer in constitutional monarchy, was to the republican. The socialist wished to have an end of masters and pin his faith in the collective intelligence of a democratic community. If they there that night did not wish to join the Socialists' ranks he would earnestly entreat them to support the Labour Electoral Association.[20]

However, the same issue of the *Workers' Republic* also reported on an 'official' meeting of the LEA presided over by the conservative trade unionist James Chambers, the President of the Trades Council. Chambers told the audience to guard against external politically motivated forces who wanted to bring 'isms' into the LEA. The LEA, according to Chambers, was to be 'non-political and non-sectarian', and was not to be 'dragged at the tail of any political party'. This was a not so veiled reference to the ISRP, which had shown such keen interest in the new organisation. It seemed that the ISRP was a lot keener on the LEA than the newly formed association was on the socialist republicans.

However, while the public organ of the ISRP hailed the formation of the LEA as a great moment in the history of the Irish working class, in private the party was aware from the very start that the LEA could eventually become a competitor for the hearts and minds of the Dublin proletariat:

> A discussion about the attitude of the LEA ensued. It seemed to be the general idea amongst our members that their attitude would be more or less hostile, and that eventually we might have to fight them.[21]

So say the minutes of the business meeting held in December 1898, a month before the local elections in which both the ISRP and the LEA were to stand candidates.

It also seems that some ISRP members had joined the LEA – evidence that the LEA had reason to fear, in its own terms, possible infiltration by the ISRP. In 1898 Edward Stewart became a member of the LEA in the North Dock Ward while at the same time being a card-carrying member of the ISRP.[22] In the weeks before the local elections of January 1899 Stewart was chosen as the ISRP's candidate for the up-coming elections and he requested support from the LEA for his candidature. This support was not forthcoming and Stewart stood as a straight ISRP candidate rather than as an LEA candidate in the North Dock Ward. He subsequently resigned from the LEA. In the weeks before the local elections, in which both groups stood candidates, Connolly referred to the LEA, as the 'main body of the army of labour', while the ISRP's members were said to be content in their role as the 'pioneers' of the labour movement.

The LEA made a breakthrough in the elections, taking seats in urban wards up and down the country. It won one-fifth of all the seats in Dublin city centre. However, its subsequent performance in local government led the ISRP to change the nature of its association with the LEA, which it saw as watering down its previously held labourite politics and, in effect, becoming nothing more than a conservative Home Rule party with a thin veneer of working-class politics at best. The LEA did not provide any distinctive working-class or labour identity at council level and its members got embroiled in factional infighting among the Home Rulers on the councils. They were also viewed as being involved in jobbery and corruption.

Less than a year after the LEA's electoral breakthrough the *Workers' Republic* gave vent to the ISRP's anger at LEA councillors' performance.

> We, like many others, confess to having been disappointed in the Labour men elected under the auspicious of the Labour Electoral Association; we did not expect that the splendid class spirit shown by the Dublin workers at the last elections would through the arrogance and weaknesses of their electoral representatives be of no practical advantage to them as a class.[23]

The ISRP had had little option but to welcome the formation of the LEA in 1898, considering the lack of a mainstream social-democratic organisation in Ireland, but the rapid change in the party's policy towards the LEA must have been a little bewildering for the membership and for the readership of the *Workers' Republic*. In the space of twelve months the LEA had apparently gone from being the 'main body of the army of labour' to nothing more than 'corrupt tools of capitalism'. While the performance of the LEA in local government had been widely criticised, the speed at which the ISRP's policy developed from critical support to outright hostility must have left some questioning its political judgement. Yet it was not only the ISRP that had been originally supportive of the LEA. Keir Hardie had welcomed the creation of the new group, but he too was disillusioned by the LEA's actions in local government. In the end, it was not so much the ISRP as the voters who decided the fate of the LEA, which was routed in the elections of 1900. Having won one-fifth of the seats on Dublin Council in January 1899, twelve months later the LEA lost most of the seats it had secured.

While the ISRP attempted during its mid-period to orientate itself to the LEA, its political engagement with the trade union movement of the time was hardly as extensive as one would imagine for a left-wing organisation. There were two principal reasons for this. First, the unions of the period were inherently conservative in nature. They were in the main craft-based unions, full of skilled workers who feared the influx of unskilled labour from the countryside into the cities, and thus often took very sectional and reactionary stances on issues. The almost revolutionary union movement of James Larkin was still some years away. The craft unions launched campaigns to protect Irish industry and saw their prime concern as being to keep the wages of their skilled workers in line with those of similar workers in Great Britain. They had little or no interest in the wider socialist cause and were in fact politically close to some of the Home Rule politicians.

The trade union movement in Ireland, such as it was in 1896, had been formed in fits and starts, resulting in the establishment of the Irish Trades Union Congress in 1894.[24] This period was marked by a surplus of labour in Ireland, with large seas of unemployment surrounding small islands of urban industrial employment. In general the unions were far from radical and not only accepted capitalism, but did not want to do anything to frighten off capital investment in the Irish economy: thus industrial peace was always to the forefront of their minds. Not surprisingly, there was friction and suspicion on both sides when it came to interaction between the ISRP and the trade union movement.

Second, the dominant theory of the international socialist movement at the time, in the form of the Second International, composed of socialist parties around the world, was that the trade union movement was fundamentally a defensive organisation of the working class. Its role was to fight on the bread-and-butter issues of wages and conditions for the proletariat it represented, but it could not be expected to question the very nature of the capitalist system. Unions intended to get the best deal they could from the capitalist class, rather than fighting for the defeat of the capitalist class itself. Many in the Second International viewed trade union activity in a dim light, on the grounds that attempts to win wage increases only postponed the day when the proletariat realised that its emancipation could only be won in a truly socialist society. Many significant figures in the international socialist movement therefore treated trade union activists with suspicion and contempt. Although union members made up a significant proportion of the German Social Democratic Party (SPD), which was then the largest and most successful left-wing party in Europe, to win the 'political' struggle, to win seats in Parliament, was shown significantly more concern by the SPD's leadership than the 'economic' demands of the unions.

Connolly and the ISRP very much took the Second International's orthodox view of the trade union movement and industrial strikes in general. On a personal level, Connolly also had much of his heritage from the British SDF weighing heavily on him when it came to strike action. The SDF, like the SPD, also believed that strikes were essentially of secondary importance in the general class struggle, with electioneering and the disseminating of socialist propaganda being of much more serious concern to socialist organisations. (In addition, the American SLP, under the leadership of Daniel De Leon, proposed the creation of radical 'socialist' trade unions to counter the more conservative trade unions that looked for only piecemeal reforms under the capitalist system.[25] That theory was to influence Connolly in later years.)

During its existence the ISRP rarely became politically involved in the industrial struggles that were happening in the capital city of the time. The writer of a letter to the *Workers' Republic* in 1898 complained about the treatment meted out to old employees by bosses in Dublin. Rather than expressing much sympathy, Connolly responded that nothing much could be done until the whole system itself was changed:

> As long as the workers are content with capitalism, they must alas be resigned to meet the same fate as other tools viz., to be cast off when worn out.[26]

This was an observation that was hardly going to win the political sympathy of that particular letter writer. During this period there were strikes by the small but growing industrial working class, particularly in Dublin, but these were by and large ignored by the ISRP. Individual members of the party did take up posts in the organised labour movement: Edward Stewart was a representative of the shop assistants on the Dublin Trades Council by 1900, while Connolly held a number of posts in the United Labourers Union, William O'Brien was active in the tailors' unions and William McLoughlin was a representative on the Trades Council for the tailors. However, because of the ISRP's belief that strikes were not fundamental to the success of socialism, the party as such was absent from activity on the picket line and tended to expend the majority of its energies in the political rather than the economic struggle.

As we have already noted, the international socialist movement was rather 'cold' on strikes and this was to remain the case until the experience of the first Russian Revolution (1905–07) had been understood by the socialist movement. The mass strike was used as a revolutionary weapon by the Russian working class and the Polish socialist Rosa Luxemburg in her pamphlet *The Mass Strike* (1906), argued that the mass strike had become an effective weapon in the class struggle, and that strikes, which seemed to have mere economic causes and aims in the beginning, were often rapidly transformed into more political struggles.[27]

> In order that the working class may participate *en masse* in any direct political action, it must first organise itself, which above all means that it must obliterate the boundaries between factories and workshops which the daily yoke of capitalism condemns it to. Therefore the mass strike is the first national spontaneous form of every great revolutionary proletarian action.[28]

Yet such insights were a number of years away for the ISRP membership, and strikes were mainly seen as a distraction for the working class, a class that should be keeping its eyes on the goal of socialism, rather than losing focus and concentrating on paltry wage rises and improved working conditions. Indeed, a series of articles by Edward Stewart in the early issues of the *Workers' Republic* are instructive here. Three articles dealing with the conditions of employment for the Dublin tram workers looked at the problems faced by the workforce as the employers attempted to radically change the conditions of work with the introduction of new machinery on the tramlines. Stewart outlines the plight of the workers in articles entitled 'Long Hours and Low Wages For the Men who Work the System', 'Conditions of Slavery Further Exposed' and 'Socialism – The Remedy'.[29] While exposing in great detail the problems faced by the tram workers, Stewart and the ISRP could offer no immediate plan of action for the workers to improve their conditions, rather a simple moral was expressed: if you want to improve your working conditions, then you have to get rid of capitalism and replace it with socialism. For example:

> Well, Companies love Unions. You know the way they encourage them and how they receive deputations from them with words of love and welcome when said deputations are seeking a redress of grievances. Never heard of it you say. Surprising. Well, I'll tell you. This particular company so loved that particular Union; one day it reared up its hind legs like a bear at a bee-hive and commenced hugging; the hugging went on for some months, till one fine day about the end of '95 or the beginning of '96 a funeral took place, and the funeral wasn't the bear's.[30]

The close attention paid by Stewart to the work and the actual living conditions of the tram workers in his trilogy of articles shows his own personal interest in trade union matters and also how he stands out after Connolly, as the second most prominent writer in the pages of the *Workers' Republic*. Stewart produced further detailed articles in the paper regarding the conditions of the boot trade in Ireland, and the relationship between dockers and their employers. More than any other member of the ISRP, Stewart was to become heavily involved in the unions during this period and was to later articulate a view within the organisation that the ISRP should become more involved in the craft union bureaucracy, in an attempt to increase its political strength and influence.

In 1900 the *Workers' Republic* turned its attention to a number of strikes involving dockers on the quays in Dublin. The strikes arose after dockworkers demanded a substantial pay increase following a restructuring of employment conditions implemented by the managers. The paper also carried a report on a docker's strike in Limerick in May 1900, calling for 'Success to the Limerick Dockers'. For the *Workers' Republic* these strikes proved that the constant state of capitalism was not one of peace, but one of war, the class war. While showing some sympathy to the workers, the official organ of the ISRP pours not a little scorn on the 'simple' trade union methods being employed by the dockers in Dublin in attempting to win their strike. The paper argues that the workers could have more power at the ballot box if they voted for a true socialist in their local ward at election time rather than the very moderate LEA member who held the North Dock seat – and that such a socialist could make a real difference to their plight, by calling for an end to all forms of wage labour:

> This is Capitalism pure and simple, and to it the workers oppose their organisation – trade unionism pure and simple. With the accent on the word 'simple'. The workers on the quay have such voting strength that they can return as their representatives on the City Council practically whoever they like, yet in the North Dock Ward their representatives are a lawyer, a publican, a shipping agent – and Alderman Fleming. It is hard to classify Alderman Fleming. He is what the Americans style a 'Labour Fakir', that is to say a man who was once a worker, and has used the labour vote to crawl into a position in a public body where the capitalist class find it to their interest to 'square' him, and use him in order to delude the working class to support capitalist nominees.[31]

Interestingly, the paper goes on to argue that strikes themselves would not even be an issue in a socialist society, as the dockers, the tailors and all the other sections of the proletariat would be their own bosses. Workers, elected by their fellow workers, would run the industries through a system of democratic workers' control:

> Under Socialism the docks and the shipping would belong to the nation, and the work would be carried on co-operatively by the

> Dockers in the public interest, under the management of men elected by the Dockers. The stevedores, instead of being tyrannical bosses over the men, would be elected from the ranks of the men for their skill in organising effectively the work required, would be the servants of the men, and all labour would be remunerated according to the full value of the work performed. Strikes would be impossible, because, as the workers would be their own bosses, there would be nobody to strike against. The Municipal Council would be an executive body representing all the industries of the city, and charged with the supervision of the industrial affairs of the population; and with the Municipal Council, and not with any private individuals, would all trades and industries require to deal in all matters affecting trade organisation, labour, and the reward of labour.[32]

This is a vivid description of how the ISRP believed a workers' state with workers' control of industry would function. (The Bolshevik government in Russia debated this very question of whether trade union organisation would be needed in a 'workers' republic' some twenty years later, in the early years after the revolution. Lenin argued in favour of the retention of the trade unions, even under a workers' government, since he believed that workers needed to have independent organisations to defend themselves from the state, no matter its political nature. Others among the Bolsheviks, such as Leon Trotsky, echoed the points made by the ISRP, arguing that trade unions had no real reason to exist under a workers' government.)

While the ISRP in theory did not believe strikes to be a weapon of much importance in the general offensive against capitalism, as we have seen, the pages of the *Workers' Republic* did carry reports on industrial unrest at the time. Yet the paper's coverage of these issues pales into insignificance when compared to its coverage of municipal elections, or the mobilisations against the Boer War, or the 1798 centenary commemorations.

During an extremely bitter Tailors strike in Dublin in May 1900 the paper did express its support for the workers, who were essentially locked out by the employers. The ISRP attempted to give some very visible and practical support to the tailors. The *Workers' Republic* of 25 May 1900 carried a brief list of the individuals and houses to which the master tailors of the City of Dublin had entrusted their work after locking out their trade union employees. The 'black-list' of eleven individuals and more than twenty houses contained exact home addresses. This was an overt act of intimidation by the ISRP towards the tailors who were breaking the strike. It was almost certain that these men's addresses would now get into the hands of those tailors who were out on strike. However, worryingly for the party a C. Martin who was on the list at 27 Wellington Quay was 'a member of the Socialist Republican Party, and is under notice of expulsion for his present conduct'.[33] This fact was made all the more embarrassing for the ISRP when it had to admit, in the following issue of the *Workers' Republic*, that they had got the address of their member C. Martin wrong, thus sending angry tailors to the house of some innocent rather than a strike breaker.

The dockers' strike in Dublin in the summer of 1900 was the industrial action followed most closely by the party and led Connolly at one time to propose a 'new departure' in the party's thinking regarding strikes. The party decided to publish a pamphlet dealing with the issue, a number of the regular public meetings held by the party focused on strikes and their role (if any) in the fight for socialism.[34] However, it is clear that the party regarded the dockers' strike as the exception rather than the norm, with the particular working conditions of the dockers and their relationship with their bosses making the exploitative nature of labour under capitalism all the clearer:

> The Dock Strike has for us certain attractions greater than most industrial disputes in Ireland. The reason being that work on the docks is carried on under thorough capitalist conditions. There the capitalist system of exploiting labour can be seen better than in most industries in this undeveloped country. There are no small employers, no working capitalists, no personal relations between masters and men. There is only one connecting link between the employers and the employees, and that link is to be found in the gold, silver, or copper coins the worker draws as the reward for his labour... The dock workers are thus pitted against a powerful combination of interests representing the entire propertied class; and the shipping companies have not only the power of their stored up capital against the poor funds of the men's union, but have also their representatives and friends in the City Council and Parliament, elected by the men themselves.[35]

The political orientation towards the dockers' strike was not indicative of the fundamental attitude of the ISRP to industrial struggles involving the Irish proletariat. Indeed, it may be the case that the interest shown by the ISRP in the dockers' struggle was mostly influenced by the fact that the strike was taking place in one of the electoral wards in which the ISRP was going to stand a candidate in January 1901.

In the main, throughout this period, and mirroring the stance taken by the majority in the Second International, the ISRP remained 'cold' on the issues of trade unions and strikes, declining to become involved in industrial unrest in any meaningful way, and contenting itself with making abstract propaganda on the need for socialism to cure all the ills of society. The Irish labour movement was to witness its own tumultuous years after the demise of the ISRP, when strikes began to take on a much more radical and political edge. If the party had survived its implosion in 1903 and 1904, and witnessed how radical syndicalism and the trade union leader James Larkin's push for 'One Big Union' excited the Irish, and particularly the Dublin working class, it might have changed its attitude and its practical policy. However, the great strikes of the Larkin period had yet to materialise and the ISRP had enough to occupy itself with when the conflict that became known as the Boer War began in South Africa in 1899.

THE BOER WAR, THE ISRP AND 'ANTI-IMPERIALISM'

War, like no other issue, has divided socialist movements over the years. At the beginning of any conflict between nations, nationalist sentiment has always been at a high level, as jingoism is used to bolster military recruitment and win over public support for war. This makes it difficult for any call for internationalist class solidarity against war to be heard. Individual socialists and socialist parties, many of whom may have been declaring their internationalism and passing anti-war resolutions for many years, are not immune to the conflict between nationalism and internationalism. This was reflected in the breakdown of the Second International in 1914, when the majority of European socialist parties came out in support of the Great War.

The onset of hostilities between the British and the independent Afrikaner republics of the Transvaal and the Orange Free State in 1899 led to a bloody conflict essentially over the diamond and gold mines of South Africa. The Boers, descendants of seventeenth-century Dutch settlers, had established both republics after advances made by the British military in the nineteenth century. In the mid-1880s gold had been found in the Transvaal and, not surprisingly, had attracted the interest of the British. Relations between the Boers and the British rapidly disintegrated from that point onwards. A number of Irish nationalists actually travelled to South Africa to fight for the Boers, but many more Irishmen fought in the colours of the British Army. The Boers were finally defeated in 1902, but not before major losses were suffered on both sides.[36]

The Boer War was thus the first major international conflict that the ISRP had to take a political stance on, and the party made its views very clear both in theory and in practice. Perceptively, Connolly had been predicting the outbreak of further international conflicts in the months before the war began. In August 1898 he wrote that: 'The influence which impels towards war is the influence of capitalism. Every war is now a capitalist move for new markets, and it is a move capitalism must make or perish.'[37] While Connolly had been focusing specifically on the possible outbreak of violence between the great imperial powers off the coast of China, there is little doubt that he believed the capitalist push for war was a worldwide phenomenon. The ISRP very much drew a connection between the rise of centralised monopoly capitalism and the growth of imperialism. This connection was made in a similar vein to Lenin's in his work *Imperialism, the Highest Stage of Capitalism* (1916).[38] While the ISRP composed its thinking and policies regarding monopolies and imperialism in the midst of a rapid intensification of capitalist development, Lenin had the benefit of historical hindsight in looking at how the very nature of capitalism in the metropolitan countries had changed in the last decade of the nineteenth century:

> This is something quite different from the old free competition between manufacturers, scattered and out of touch with one another, and producing for an unknown market. Concentration has reached the point at which it is possible to make an approximate estimate of all sources of raw materials (for example, the iron ore deposits) of a country and even, as we shall see, of several countries, or of the whole world. Not only are such estimates made, but these sources are captured by gigantic monopolist associations. An approximate estimate of the capacity of markets is also made, and the associations 'divide' them up amongst themselves by agreement. Skilled labour is monopolised, the best engineers are engaged; the means of transport are captured — railways in America, shipping companies in Europe and America. Capitalism in its imperialist stage leads directly to the most comprehensive socialisation of production; it, so to speak, drags the capitalists, against their will and consciousness, into some sort of a new social order, a transitional one from complete free competition to complete socialisation.[39]

It is to the credit of the ISRP, and of Connolly in particular, that the party was able to understand the changes occurring in capitalism, and the importance of the rise in imperialism in 1899, in a way similar to Lenin's considered views of 1916. Others in the European socialist movement, principally the Polish socialist Rosa Luxemburg, were also making the link between conflict and the rise in militarism among the major imperialist powers in the 1890s.

The ISRP welcomed the replacement by monopoly capitalism of the more varied and competitive free market, full of much smaller capitalist firms, that had dominated the international economy until the 1880s. The ISRP believed that it was taking the

> absolutely correct position that the crushing out of small capitalists by large ones will tend to increase the ranks of the working class, concentrate industry under a centralised management, decrease the numbers of those interested in private property, and so make the ultimate attainment of Socialism easier.[40]

Nevertheless, the ISRP also took a dialectical approach by arguing that it was the pernicious results of this centralisation, such as war, that made the need for socialism ever more pressing. The phase of imperialism, which really began in the late 1880s, also saw the concentration and centralisation of capitalism take place in a wide variety of areas of the economy. The monopolies that were created controlled large proportions of their markets and as a result of this came the phenomenon of 'surplus capital' in the metropolitan countries. The imperialist era of capitalism is marked by this existence of surplus capital in the hands of a small number of monopolies in the advanced nations, the export of capital to the underdeveloped world becoming an important element. The drive for new markets, the appearance of powerful, privately owned and politically motivated monopolies, and the rise in tension between the 'imperialist powers' meant that war was almost inevitable during this period.[41]

Thus the strong 'anti-imperialist' line that the ISRP took during the Boer conflict did not just emanate from the party's opposition to the British Empire's control over Ireland, but also from a theoretical position that saw the violence and misery produced by international wars as fundamental consequences of the continued growth of international capitalism. Almost expecting the predictable attacks from some on the British left, who said that the ISRP's opposition to the British during the Boer War came from petty-nationalist anti-British sentiment, the ISRP made it clear that this was not the case.

> Is this hostility to the British Empire due to the fact of our national and racial subjection by that power, and does it exist in spite of our Socialism, or is it consistent with the doctrines we hold as adherents of the Marxist propaganda, and believers in the Marxist economics.[42]

The ISRP made clear that its stance regarding the war came very much from the latter source, a strong 'scientific socialist' outlook.

The Boers were not supported by the ISRP because of the former's politics. Indeed, the politicians of the republics, many of whom were conservative, Calvinist and racist towards the African natives thus hardly made them natural allies of the radical socialist. The British were to be opposed because to take a stand against the British Empire was to take a stand against imperialism and the forces of capitalism. A military defeat for the British Empire in South Africa would not just be a blow for British capitalism and a victory for the people of the Boer republics, but it would also forward the cause of socialism in Britain, according to the logic of the ISRP's argument. Its anti-imperialism arose from an essentially economic view of imperialism, rather than principally a moral stand against the powerful military hold the British Empire extended across much of the globe. The ISRP believed

> that as colonial expansion and the conquest of new markets are necessary for the prolongation of the life of capitalism, the prevention of colonial expansion and the loss of markets to countries capitalistically developed, such as England, precipitates economic crises there, and so gives an impulse to revolutionary thought and helps to shorten the period required to develop backward countries and thus prepare the economic conditions needed for our triumph.[43]

The ISRP campaigned against the British Empire's conduct in South Africa throughout the conflict, holding public meetings, organising major demonstrations and printing literature denouncing the British Empire. The ISRP took what would be later termed (with regards to the First World War) a 'revolutionary defeatist' line, welcoming the possible defeat of the British Empire in Africa and seeing the opportunities for forces who were against the Empire in Ireland to build their influence within the Irish working class. Right from the beginning of the conflict the *Workers' Republic* openly opposed the British intervention as nothing more than the expression of military might by a greedy capitalist power extending and deepening its influence in a foreign land:

> At the time of going to press it seems probable that in a few weeks at most the British Government will have declared war against the South African Republic[s]. Ostensibly in pursuance of a chivalrous desire to obtain political concessions in their adopted country for British citizens anxious to renounce their citizenship, but in reality for the purpose of enabling an unscrupulous gang of capitalists to get into their hands the immense riches of the diamond fields. Such a war will undoubtedly take rank as one of the most iniquitous wars of the century. No better corroboration of the truth of the socialist maxim that the modern state is but a committee of rich men administering public affairs in the interest of the upper class, has been afforded of late years, than is furnished by this spectacle of a gang of South African speculators setting in motion the whole machinery of the British Empire in furtherance of their own private ends.[44]

While aware of the international context of the conflict the ISRP and Connolly also believed that the Boer War highlighted telling truths about Irish politics at the time. The ISRP believed that the conflict proved that, despite all the talk among 'advanced nationalists' about the importance of Ireland on the international scene, Britain could move large numbers of her troops from the island to Africa with little fear of any uprising or major discontent among its Irish subjects: 'The British Government has no fears on the score of Ireland; the Home Rule Party, and their good friends the Constabulary, may be trusted to keep this country quiet.'[45] In a socialistic spin on the old refrain that 'England's problem is Ireland's opportunity', the ISRP outlined how it thought the Boer War could be taken advantage of to advance the cause of socialism and national liberation in Ireland:

> ...if the working class of Ireland were only united and understood their power sufficiently well, and had shaken off their backs the Home Rule–Unionist twin brethren keeping us apart that their class may rob us, they would see in this complication a chance for making a long step forward towards better conditions of life and, seeing it, act upon it in a manner that would ensure the absence from the Transvaal of a considerable portion of the British army. The class-conscious workers who chafe under our present impotence, and long to remove it, will find the path pointed out to them in the ranks of the Irish Socialist Republican Party.[46]

Showing that their ideas did not just remain in the realm of theory, the ISRP began to campaign actively against the war and attempted to build a mass movement in opposition to the conflict. The ISRP worked closely with republican groups in opposition to the war within the newly established Irish Transvaal Committee. The committee was formed by republicans, at a meeting presided over by Maud Gonne on 10 October 1899, as a cross-party organisation and won the support of such people as Arthur Griffith, Michael Davitt and William O'Brien MP. Yet even before the creation of the committee the first anti-war meeting had been instigated by the ISRP and held in Foster Place Dublin on 27 August. The meeting, which was reportedly well-attended, was addressed by Connolly himself, while Maud Gonne, invited to speak, had sent her apologies. She was to work shoulder-to-shoulder with the ISRP during the agitation against the Boer War and came close to joining the organisation.

At the committee's meeting on 10 October a resolution of sympathy for the Boer republic was passed. The resolution outlined the British Empire's role across the globe in India, Egypt and Ireland, where its government was 'maintained upon the bayonets of an occupying army against the will of the people', and denounced the 'interference of the British capitalist government in the internal affairs of the Transvaal Republic as an act of criminal aggression, wishes long life to the Republic, and trusts that our fellow-countrymen will, if need be, take up arms in defence of their adopted country'.[47] While reporting the resolution the *Workers' Republic* also rather sarcastically contrasted the lack of military opposition in Ireland to the British Empire with the opposition in other nations across the globe, including the Boer republics.

> The British Army is getting its hands full in South Africa. The defeated, demoralised, disheartened, subjugated, routed, dispersed, conquered, disarmed and humiliated Boers are still toppling over British battalions, capturing British convoys, cutting British lines of communication, and keeping Lord Roberts and all his generals in a state of almighty panic and unrest, and not a single soldier can be spared from South Africa for a long time to come. The Boxers in China have developed a sudden aptitude for war, are prowling around on the hunt for foreign devils, and with a smile that is child-like and bland are offering to box all Europe, with Japan and America thrown in as appetisers. Great Britain is in want of soldiers there also. Now it only wants a native rising in India, and then would come our Irish opportunity. With war in Africa, war in China, war in India, we of the unconquered Celtic race would rise up in our millions from Malin Head to Cape Clear, from Dublin to Galway, and – and well, pass 'strong' resolutions, and then go home

and pray that somebody else may beat the Sasanach. The Boers are invulnerable on kopjes, the Boxers are death on missionaries, but we are irresistible on 'resolutions'.[48]

A number of public demonstrations were also held in Dublin against the aggression of the British Empire and calling for a victory for the Boers. A meeting later in 1899 on Dublin's Northside attracted an impressive crowd of some 2,000 and was attended by Maud Gonne. This event was to go down as one of the high points in the history of the ISRP, as it proved to be a major mobilisation on the part of the small organisation, as well as an embarrassment to the authorities. At the meeting in Beresford Place (recorded in almost breathless detail in an article entitled 'Diary of the Troubles' in the *Workers' Republic*)[49] the protestors were baton-charged by police. After the open-air meeting the police raided the offices of the ISRP, where they took 'one Red Flag, one Green Flag, two Boer Flags, and the Historic Black Flag which led the anti-Jubilee procession of 1897'. The *Workers' Republic* was suspended for one week 'owing to disorganisation caused by above events'. Connolly was arrested during the disturbances and fined two pounds on pain of one month's imprisonment, and had to find bail in the sum of ten pounds or go to prison for another month. The bail was paid and Connolly was released. The rest of 1899 and the early months of 1900 saw the ISRP carry on a high level of anti-war activity, with marches, public meetings and further protests taking place in Dublin.

There has been some speculation as to whether Connolly contemplated organising an Irish insurrection during the Boer War.[50] There is little doubt that he was very optimistic about the damage that the conflict was going to inflict on the British Empire. Writing in November 1899 he seemed to be itching to begin composing a political obituary for the empire he hated so completely:

> Well I think it is the beginning of the end. This great blustering British Empire; this Empire of truculent bullies, is rushing headlong to its doom. Whether they ultimately win or lose, the Boers have pricked the bubble of England's fighting reputation.[51]

It was against this backdrop of Connolly's belief that the British Empire was facing major, possibly fatal, difficulties that he may have discussed an Irish insurrection with the editor of the *United Irishman*, and future founder of Sinn Féin, Arthur Griffith. Evidence is sketchy at best and, although Connolly in his writings for the *Workers'*

Republic, obviously believed that the objective conditions for a military blow against the British were increasing all the time, the subjective weakness of the anti-British forces in Ireland make such speculation just that and no more.

The evidence, such as it is, comes from a somewhat unreliable source in any case. George Lyons was a colleague and political disciple of Arthur Griffith. In 1923 he published a book *Some Recollections of Griffith and his Times*. Much of it is written in dialogue form. Whether Lyons could have remembered conversations that took place sometimes three decades earlier in such perfect detail must be questioned. The book is also little more than a hagiography of Griffith and his politics. Griffith is described as the 'Moses' of the Irish people who had led them to the Promised Land. Lyons is also very hostile to socialism and defends Griffith from some of the mild attacks launched against him by Connolly. Lyons claims that after a meeting of the Transvaal Committee in 1899 Connolly approached Griffith with revolution on his mind:

> That night, on the way home, James Connolly had a suggestion to offer. England was strained to the utmost, there were only 25,000 of their troops in Ireland, it would not take much to overcome this garrison. That point was conceded.
> He then unfolded a plan for capturing of buildings in Dublin City, fortifying them as best we could and proclaiming a Republic in the belief that the country would rise spontaneously. Griffith pointed out that there were not 500 nationalists in Dublin armed with revolvers at the time. 'Have your revolution first and the arms will come afterwards', exclaimed Connolly. Griffith objected. Connolly went home in a 'huff'.[52]

As already stated, there are a number of reasons to question the accuracy of this account, although the general argument made by Connolly in this account does chime somewhat with what he was writing in the pages of the *Workers' Republic* at the time. Connolly did believe that the armies of the British Empire were spreading themselves thin and were in a weak state in Ireland. Yet it is very unlikely that he seriously considered organising an armed rebellion. There is no discussion of such a plan in the minutes of the ISRP's meetings and neither William O'Brien nor any other of the party's former members mention it in their writings after the demise of the party.

It is intriguing to note the similarity between the plans for the rising described by Connolly in this alleged conversation with Griffith and what eventually happened two decades later, in 1916.

Connolly had few men in the ISRP and they had little or no military training between them, while the advanced nationalist military men in the Irish Republican Brotherhood had not been in full-scale action since 1868 and had seen their membership fall since that failed uprising. Although Britain was moving many of her troops from the island to continue her actions in South Africa, it is extremely unlikely that any attempted anti-British insurrection would have been successful in Ireland in 1899, despite the pro-Boer sentiment that was undoubtedly widespread at the time.

While talk of insurrection was not matched by any action, the campaign against the Boer War in which the ISRP played a central role did show that Britain could not rely on total support from the Irish population. It ensured that Ireland could not be seen as a loyal follower of British foreign policy. A substantial section of the Irish population made it clear that they were not in favour of Britain's continued prosecution of the war in the Boer republics. The ISRP flew the flag of anti-imperialism throughout the conflict and made the connection between imperialism, capitalism and war, a connection that many socialists both in Great Britain and in continental Europe not only failed to make during the Boer War, but also less than two decades later, before the outbreak of the First World War in 1914.

NOTES

1. The *Workers' Republic* (*WR*) was relaunched in 1914 by the Socialist Party of Ireland, and another version of paper came out in the 1920s, this time published by the Communist Party of Ireland. However, whenever we refer to the *Workers' Republic* in this study we are referring to the paper published by the ISRP between August 1898 and May 1903.
2. William O'Brien, *Forth the Banners Go* (Dublin: Three Candles, 1969), p. 10.
3. *WR*, Vol. 1, No. 1, 13 Aug. 1898.
4. *WR*, Vol. 4, No. 22, 15 Dec. 1900.
5. *WR*, Vol. 2, No. 20, 21 Oct. 1899.
6. *WR*, Vol. 1, No. 3, 27 Aug. 1898.
7. Most recently reprinted as James Connolly, *Labour in Irish History* (London: Bookmarks, 1987).
8. *WR*, Vol. 1, No. 9, 8 Oct. 1898.
9. *WR*, Vol. 3, No. 3, 12 May 1900.
10. *WR*, Vol. 3, No. 5, 16 June 1900.
11. *WR*, Vol. 2, No. 1, 5 May 1899.
12. *WR*, Vol. 2, No. 15, 7 Oct. 1899.
13. *WR*, Vol. 5, No. 9, April 1903.
14. *WR*, Vol. 2, No. 20, 21 Oct. 1899.

15. See V.I. Lenin, *What is to be Done?* (Moscow: Progress Publishers, 1973).
16. V.I.Lenin, *Collected Works*, Vol. 5. (Moscow: Progress Publishers, 1973), pp. 22–3.
17. *WR*, Vol. 5, No. 2, Aug. 1902.
18. *WR*, Vol. 1, No. 3, 27 Aug. 1898.
19. *WR*, Vol. 1, No. 3, 27 Aug. 1898.
20. *WR*, Vol. 1, No. 9, 8 Oct. 1898.
21. Minutes, 19 Dec. 1898, in Minutes of the Irish Socialist Republican Party, 1898–1904, MS 16264–67, O'Brien Collection, National Library of Ireland (NLI).
22. O'Brien, *Forth the Banners Go*, p. 31.
23. *WR*, Vol. 2, No. 16, 14 Oct. 1899.
24. F.S.L. Lyons, *Ireland Since the Famine* (London: Fontana Press, 1985), pp. 271–2.
25. See James Joll, *The Second International* (London: Weidenfield & Nicolson, 1955).
26. *WR*, Vol. 1, No. 5, 10 Sept. 1898. William Bradshaw also referred rather disparagingly to strikes as examples of the 'incoherent class struggle': *WR*, Vol. 3, No. 1, May 1900.
27. See Rosa Luxemburg, 'The Mass Strike', reprinted in Mary-Alice Waters (ed.) *Rosa Luxemburg Speaks* (New York: Pathfinder Press, 1970).
28. Rosa Luxemburg, quoted in Tony Cliff, *Rosa Luxemburg* (London: Bookmarks, 1986), p. 35.
29. *WR*, Vol. 1, No. 1, 13 Aug. 1898, *WR*, Vol. 1, No. 2, 20 Aug. 1898, *WR*, Vol. 1, No. 3, 27 Aug. 1898.
30. *WR*, Vol. 1, No. 2, 20 Aug. 1898.
31. *WR*, Vol. 3, No. 9, 15 July 1900.
32. Ibid.
33. *WR*, Vol. 3, No. 3, 25 May 1900.
34. Minutes, 10 July 1900 and 17 July 1900. The party would take a decisive decision on trade unions at a meeting on 4 September 1903. The ISRP voted to 'debar trade union officials from membership (of the ISRP)'. Letter, Thomas Brady to James Connolly (no date), February 1904. William O'Brien MS (NLI) 15,674 Folder (6).
35. *WR*, Vol. 3, No. 9, 15 July 1900.
36. See Thomas Pakenham, *The Boer War* (New York: Random House, 1979).
37. *WR*, Vol. 1, No. 2, 20 Aug. 1898.
38. See V.I. Lenin, *Imperialism, the Highest Stage of Capitalism* (Moscow: Progress Publishers, 1983).
39. Ibid., pp. 10–11.
40. *WR*, Vol. 2, No. 20, 21 Oct 1899.
41. See Ernest Mandel, *Introduction to Marxism* (London: Ink Links, 1979), pp. 63–7.
42. *WR*, Vol. 2, No. 22, 4 Nov. 1899.
43. *WR*, Vol. 2, No. 20, 21 Oct. 1899.
44. *WR*, Vol. 2, No. 12, 19 Aug. 1899.
45. Ibid.
46. Ibid.

47. *WR*, Vol. 3, No. 7, 30 June 1900.
48. Ibid.
49. *WR*, Vol. 2, No. 28, 30 Dec. 1899.
50. For example, in K.B. Nowlan, *The Making of 1916: Studies in the History of the Rising* (Dublin: Stationery Office, 1969), p. 190, note 15, as quoted in W.K. Anderson, *James Connolly and the Irish Left* (Dublin: Irish Academic Press, 1994), p. 165.
51. *WR*, Vol. 2, No. 23, 18 Nov. 1899.
52. George Lyons, *Some Recollections of Griffith and his Times* (Dublin: Talbot Press, 1923), pp. 13–14.

CHAPTER THREE

Elections and Beyond, 1900–02

The British Parliament passed the Local Government Act in 1898. This important piece of legislation resulted in the further extension of the electoral franchise and helped to break the stranglehold that the landlords had had over the old grand jury system in municipal politics. The Act led to a radical upheaval in politics at the local level and allowed the ISRP to enter the electoral field for the first time in the local elections of January 1899.[1]

The Act has traditionally been seen as part of the British government's rather optimistic plan of 'killing Home Rule with kindness', or more specifically the 'Constructive Unionism' articulated by Joseph Chamberlain, MP for Birmingham and (at that time) leader of the radical wing of the Liberal Party. He believed that the best way to appease Ireland was to provide some form of local government that would help to placate the more radical separatist feelings growing among the population. He was extremely close to unionist thinking and wanted to prevent any form of radical Home Rule being established in Ireland. The idea that the ISRP could have benefited from anything that Chamberlain had campaigned for is ironic. Chamberlain was one of the party's chief hate figures: when he received an honorary doctorate at Trinity College, Dublin, in December 1899, the ISRP held a noisy picket at the gates of Trinity to protest against Chamberlain's views on Ireland and his support for the British war effort in the Boer conflict.[2]

In reality the ISRP had little to worry about, because this progressive piece of legislation was really introduced as a result of pressure applied by the trade unions in Ireland and Great Britain during the 1890s, not because of the political patronage of

Chamberlain. The Irish Trades Union Congress (ITUC) had passed a resolution in 1894 calling for an extension of the franchise. Many union members, who tended to be skilled craft workers, now wanted to have a say at the local level. The Act was also part of a much broader sweep of progressive legislation on the franchise that was just beginning to be introduced because of the pressure for it applied by the British labour movement.

In practice the Act helped replace the old system of grand juries with elected urban and county councils. These councils were responsible for roads, housing, public health and the Poor Law. All these were policy areas in which an elected socialist with a left-wing municipal programme could have made a significant impact.

Elections became a central component of the work carried out by the ISRP following the introduction of the Act. In total the ISRP stood in eight separate elections during the years 1899–1903 restricting itself to Dublin city centre wards. While the extension of the franchise had been welcomed by the ISRP as an opportunity to bring its politics to a wider audience, in stark contrast the larger (although still split) Home Rule Party worried about the threat that it could pose to its power base. Always happy to have a dig at one of the leading lights of the Home Rulers, John Redmond, who was destined to become the leader of the reunited Home Rule Party in 1900, the *Workers' Republic* tried to highlight how Redmond had attempted to block the growth of the labour movement following the passage of the Act:

> He is the gentleman who, when the Irish Working Class first got the Municipal franchise granted them in 1898, stumped this country asking the workers to vote for landlords to represent them – in order, he said, to show the English people that we would not make a revolutionary use of our power. The Irish working class answered him by forming independent Labour Electoral organisations, and sending landlords and middle class Home Rulers alike about their business.[3]

Despite the emphasis that the ISRP placed on electoral work, the results at the polls proved to be a continued source of disappointment. Its candidates were not elected in any ward in any of the elections they contested. This failure was painful for the small party. The party's programme of 1896 specified how critical electoral success was to the ISRP's overall political strategy:

> the conquest by the Social Democracy of political power in

Parliament, and on all public bodies in Ireland, is the readiest and most effective means whereby the revolutionary forces may be organised to attain that end.[4]

Indeed, electoral work was seen as more important than the publication of the *Workers' Republic,* which invariably failed to appear during the months and weeks preceding election days. When the resources of the ISRP were pushed to the limit, it was the paper that suffered as all the party's finances were put into fighting an election campaign. While the ISRP failed at the ballot box, it had to sit back and watch other political entities, such as the LEA, have almost instant success at the polls. Yet Connolly still believed that the whole effort was worth it, as it helped to raise the profile of the party:

> We did not win any seats at the elections, but we crowded more propaganda into the two months they lasted than during any ten months in our previous history.[5]

It was with some optimism and excitement that the party decided to stand its first candidate in the elections of January 1899. The *Workers' Republic* of October 1898 carried an article entitled 'A Socialist Candidate for Dublin Corporation' declaring:

> The Social Republicans of Ireland step at last from the domain of theory into the realm of practice. The Class War enters upon its final political expression. Comrades: To your posts.[6]

The decision to stand candidates in local elections was not taken without some extensive discussion within the party, highlighting the fact that not every member was as enthusiastic about the party's involvement as the anonymous writer of that article was. The motion to stand Edward Stewart in the election was moved at a party meeting in October 1898:

> This motion was productive of a protracted discussion which was participated in by nearly every member present. The motion, however, was finally passed and Comrade Stewart was elected to contest the seat.[7]

Edward Stewart was thus confirmed as the party's candidate in the North Dock Ward in Dublin.

The election allowed the ISRP to bring its politics to a much wider audience than usual in this predominantly working-class ward.

According to the party minutes, over 1,000 envelopes containing election literature and Stewart's municipal manifesto were delivered to homes throughout the ward. The party threw itself fully into the campaign. The North Dock Ward seemed eminently suitable for the ISRP to campaign in, as it included the area of the docks where the party had built up some limited contacts with workers. The ward reached from the East Wall to Beresford Place, where the ISRP held a number of public meetings, and all the way to the upper end of Sheriff Street. In the course of the election some underhand tactics on the part of the ISRP's opponents were evident. A public meeting held by Stewart in the ward a month before the poll was marred by constant heckling from a group in the crowd and some seemingly well-coordinated scuffles at the fringes. It should be borne in mind, however, that the party tended to overhype such tactics out of all proportion, to help to provide excuses for its continued failure at the polls.

In the end Stewart received a modest yet respectable 448 votes, falling just over 150 votes short of winning a seat. The LEA's candidate, a Mr Fleming, topped the poll and three Home Rule candidates followed him into office. Despite this failure the ISRP was rather buoyant about its result and one member, William Bradshaw, wrote an article for the mainstream Dublin press (principally the *Evening Herald*, which printed Bradshaw's article in full) displaying his own ability at late nineteenth-century political spin:

> It was from the latter [the LEA] we received the greatest opposition (underhand, because they were afraid to attack in the open), as they had all the prejudice on their side. However, you will be surprised to learn that notwithstanding all obstacles, there was a phenomenal poll in favour of Stewart, which promises well for the cause of Socialism in Ireland.[8]

Bradshaw also pointed out that one in three voters had voted for Stewart (voters could vote for up to four candidates). Yet, whatever the favourable spin, Stewart was defeated at the polls. The election saw the broad left make a number of advances across Ireland when the LEA polled well in Limerick, Dundalk, Waterford, Castlebar and Belfast. In Dublin the LEA fielded more than ten candidates and after the results were counted it held (as we have seen) one-fifth of the council seats in the capital city.[9] In the months before the election the ISRP had sought an endorsement from the LEA for its candidate. This endorsement was not, of course, forthcoming.[10]

The ISRP also turned its ire on the newly constituted United Irish League (UIL) which had stood candidates against the ISRP:

> The United Irish Leaguers have supported the Socialist candidate at North East Lanark in Scotland, and are supporting the Socialist candidate at Dewsbury, England; in opposing Socialist candidates in Dublin they are only acting in the inconsistent and treacherous manner that has marked their history from the beginning.[11]

The UIL had been formed in 1898 by William O'Brien MP as a movement calling for peasant ownership of the land and the introduction of other progressive reforms in agriculture. The League had built a small number of branches among the Irish communities in both England and Scotland. O'Brien (not to be confused with his namesake, a member of the ISRP) had formerly been a member of the Land League and had spent time in Kilmainham Prison alongside Parnell in 1881. The formation of the UIL and the extension of the franchise gave a major impetus to the reunification of the Irish parliamentary factions in 1900. The threat from the UIL and the fear that their political hegemony was being undermined by other political groupings in municipal politics helped to concentrate the minds of the divided Home Rule leaders, and led to the re-formation of their party under the leadership of John Redmond.[12]

Elections gave the ISRP an opportunity to publish its municipal programme, which was meant to be a concrete description of socialist principles for use in local government. The influence of the party's official set of ten 'minimum' demands in the programme of 1896 can also be seen in each of its municipal manifestos. The various programmes for the different wards in which the party stood candidates over the years differed little from each election to the next. The programmes all called for an eight-hour day to be introduced for Dublin Corporation employees, as well as one week's leave each year. The programme, if implemented, would have seen the introduction of a minimum wage of six pence an hour for all Corporation employees. The ISRP also encouraged proposals to erect more workers' dwellings and to create municipal coal yards, to be maintained by the Corporation, where local residents could purchase coal at cost price, thus saving the 'middle man's profits'. The municipal programme also called for National School buildings to be made available to local groups for meetings after school hours. The lack of public premises suitable for meetings was something that the ISRP was all too aware of.

With such proposals for gradual democratisation of the instruments of local government and an overt intention to look after the working class's economic needs, the municipal programme of the ISRP was clearly socialist in nature and was sharply to the left of the LEA's policies. The latter reflected the interests of the relatively conservative craft unions, which were principally concerned with protecting the livelihoods of skilled workers in Dublin. The programme of the LEA called for very limited piecemeal reforms, while the stand taken by the ISRP was to present reform 'as a means of organising the forces of democracy for revolution'.[13]

The ISRP decided in late 1899 to stand Stewart in the North Dock Ward once again in the elections of January 1900. This decision was taken following his 'magnificent poll in the last election', as the *Workers' Republic* put it enthusiastically.[14] By this stage the ISRP had moved sharply away from supporting the LEA, after what it saw as the LEA's betrayal of the working-class electorate after it reached office. The ISRP felt that the LEA's members had not helped to advance the cause of labour during their time in office. The ISRP was contemplating standing more than one candidate in the elections of 1900, but it had to consider the tactics the LEA was likely to deploy:

> It all depends upon whether certain people masquerading as representatives of Labour are wise enough to know their place. If they don't know their place, it may become necessary to put up against their leaders, a candidate who will teach them. You see the Labour Electoral Association was useful as a stop-gap, a mere temporary expedient.[15]

To help to boil the anger of the party further, the LEA decided to stand a candidate in the North Dock Ward too. Its candidate, a Mr Bergin, was an 'employer and a publican', as the *Workers' Republic* declared sniffily.[16] In a 180-degree political swing from twelve months before, the LEA had now become the political enemy of the ISRP and the major target for its polemical venom: 'With this band of intellectual weaklings and corrupt tools of capitalism the LEA declares in favour of an employer and against the worker.'[17]

In a bitter contest Stewart, who had his electoral address to the North Dock Ward printed in the *Workers' Republic* in December 1899, had to stand down as the candidate just weeks before the poll. In an incident that presaged many more such problems that the party was to have with election candidates, Stewart was found by the authorities to have been struck off the electoral roll. After the opposition had highlighted this, Stewart was disqualified from standing in the election. The party raised the matter with the Town Clerk, but Murtagh Lyng concluded that, 'as far as he could gather, Stewart had been disqualified through being reported dead or some similar trick'.[18] At the last moment Murtagh Lyng stepped in as the ISRP's candidate, but a combination of disastrous preparation and the labour vote being squeezed because of a major swing against the LEA meant that the ISRP polled much lower than in the previous election in the ward. The elections, which occurred against the backdrop of an outbreak of typhoid in working-class Dublin, witnessed a more general backlash against labour candidates across the country, as the voting public turned against the LEA after their performance in local government over the previous year. Connolly himself called it the 'municipal backwash': in the elections of 1899 the word 'labour' had given a major boost to any candidate, while in 1900 the word brought disaster upon all who stood for election under its banners'.

> We must remember that the municipal backwash of this year was the almost inevitable result of the disappointment felt by the public at the miserable intrigues and squalid squabbling with which the Labour Party in the Council had signalised their years of office.[19]

Voters held the whole of the political left culpable for the lack of effectiveness and the corruption of the LEA while in office. The newly formed UIL as well as the recently reunified Home Rule Party gained the advantage in local government. This setback for the labour movement in Ireland should not be underestimated. The introduction of the Local Government Act had brought a variant of 'home rule' to the local political scene and the UIL, the Home Rulers and the 'advanced nationalist' groups who began to take control of local bodies moved themselves into important positions of political power. Grappling with the political and ideological problems posed by failure at the polls, Connolly tended to react in angry defiance rather than providing any considered analysis:

> We shall fight again, fight until we have the majority of the workers on our side knowing that when we do have the majority, as have it we will, all the purchased votes of the residuum will not save the capitalists.[20]

These municipal bodies proved to be significant springboards and training grounds for political leaders who then moved into politics at the national level. Local government was a perfect position from which to gain experience and to build a political support base. Because of the perception of the left among the voting public, created mainly by the LEA's performance in local government from 1899 to 1900, labour candidates failed to gain or hold seats in urban and rural wards alike. Labour was already one step behind its opponents in these crucial early years of local politics in Ireland.

Thus a difficult relationship between the ISRP and election campaigns had begun. In its propaganda the ISRP tended to blame 'dirty tricks' on the part of opponents as the principal reason for its heavy and repeated defeats at the polls in local elections. It was undoubtedly true that underhand tactics were not unknown in local elections in Dublin, particularly in the early years of the new system, as working-class areas of the city were very inexperienced in the ways of free elections. Members of the UIL and the Home Rule Party did indeed 'buy' votes by promising voters drinks. However, the constant cry from the ISRP about dirty deeds by their rivals began to wear thin with party members, unhappy with the continued failure at election time.

In January 1901 William McLoughlin, a member of the Tailors Society of Dublin stood for the ISRP in the North City Ward. He won 314 seats and came within 97 votes of ousting the Home Rule candidate. More worryingly for the party, in the weeks before the elections of 1901 it was engulfed by an internal row, essentially about party strategy.

The row arose after two party members on the Dublin Trades Council, Edward Stewart and William McLoughlin voted in favour of the Council endorsing the candidature of a Conservative, a Mr Richardson. In the run-up to the elections, disagreement broke out at the party's weekly business meetings. Connolly raised his concerns regarding information he had received that seemed to indicate that both Stewart and McLoughlin supported a Tory candidate. The report in the sometimes dry party minutes gives some indication of the ferocity of argument within the ISRP that was sparked by this incident. The row was also indicative of more fundamental problems under the surface within the ISRP, problems that eventually saw the organisation implode in 1903 and 1904.[21]

McLoughlin admitted that he had supported Richardson on the Trades Council. He asserted that he had attended a meeting of the Tailors Society, which he represented on the Council, members of that union had called for him to vote for Richardson. McLoughlin argued that he was on the Trades Council as a tailors' representative not as a socialist republican, and thus was 'acting on the mandate of his trade, not on his own convictions'. Dan O'Brien said that McLoughlin should have resigned his post on the Council rather than voting for the Tory candidate, who was apparently known for his 'flunkeyism'.

Stewart's stated reasons for voting for Richardson on the Trades Council are perhaps even more enlightening considering his future role in the eventual split in the ISRP. Combining incipient reformism with a deft grasp of political sectarianism, Stewart essentially defended his actions by reasoning that the real enemies of the ISRP on the Trades Council were now the LEA and the UIL, not the Home Rulers or the Tories. Believing that what little influence McLoughlin and he himself held on the Trades Council emanated from the existence of numerous factions that were all in relatively weak states, Stewart said that he would do anything to oppose the LEA, 'even if he had to vote Tory'.

William Bradshaw accused Stewart of political sophistry, arguing that he did not believe that a socialist could be forwarding the cause of workers by voting for a Tory. Even in a tactical sense, Bradshaw said, the ISRP was bound to suffer from a Tory reactionary vote. Despite the protestations of Connolly, William O'Brien and Bradshaw, a motion absolving the two Trades Council representatives of any wrongdoing in their actions was passed by a majority of the ISRP's members. As this incident makes clear, a number of the ISRP's members involved in trade union politics had become more interested in petty factional intrigue within the bureaucracy than in propagating an openly socialist agenda.

The continued failure of the party at the polls meant that some of the membership became disillusioned, and turned to futile political sectarianism and factional squabbles, principally in the form of disputes with the LEA. The fact that the ISRP could be seen to have given support to the sponsorship of a Tory electoral candidate on the Trades Council must have confused anybody standing outside the organisation. The row was certainly a source of deep embarrassment for Connolly himself.

While these problems continued behind the scenes, the public face of the ISRP, in the form of continuing defeats at the polls, was very much on show. In the pages of the *Workers' Republic* Connolly accused the party's electoral opponents of literally buying votes by buying voters drinks.

Looking back many years after the event, William O'Brien said that there was little doubt that drink played a part in the municipal politics of Dublin, inexperienced as it was with the culture of open elections. It was a city crippled by poverty and chronic alcoholism, perfect ground on which dirty electoral tricks could prosper:

> As regards elections in those years, almost everyone had or could have a vote and when the election day came around the public-houses supporting the United Irish League candidates gave plenty of free drinks, and this got votes for them.[22]

However, drink and dirty tricks could not have been the only source of the ISRP's failure at the polling booths. The historian Mary Daly agrees that drink obviously played a role in municipal elections of the period, but concludes that to 'attribute nationalist success solely to the value of free drink and control of tenement property is somewhat naïve'. Daly believes that the ability of the 'all-embracing' Home Rule Party to sell itself as a friend of labour, combined with the inability of the LEA to create a clear and effective opposition at the municipal level, were much more significant factors contributing to the failure of the left to win a substantial number of seats at local elections.[23]

Whatever role the 'demon drink' played in the failure of the ISRP to make an impact at election time, the electoral registration process that took place in the months before elections undoubtedly favoured the larger, more conservative parties. Election workers for the Home Rule Party and the UIL set about trying to get people who might have been sympathetic to the ISRP struck off the voting register, much as had happened to Edward Stewart before the election in January 1900. Decades after the event William O'Brien explained why he believed that the registration process had made it difficult for him and his comrades to make an impact at local elections. The party's failure at the polls, according to O'Brien,

> was mainly due to the fact that registration work was looked after by the paid agents appointed by the different political parties. They put on applicants for the vote and unless somebody had an interest in fighting these applications they went on automatically, whereas in addition to that they objected to a large number of people they thought would not be favourable to their own party and unless these people fought the objection, which in many cases they did not, they were struck off. So the whole thing was pretty unsatisfactory.[24]

In January 1902 the ISRP had its most successful electoral result when it received a combined total of more than 800 votes in three electoral wards. The results may be partially explained by the endorsement of its candidates by the Dublin Trades Council and of Connolly by his own union, the United Labourers, for his candidature in the Wood Quay Ward. The endorsement by the Trades Council reflected the growing influence of the party on the union scene in the capital. Stewart, Connolly and McLoughlin were all members of the executive Trades Council and were building alliances with some of the non-aligned members of the Council. This gave the party some brief hope of an electoral breakthrough in the Dublin area. Connolly won 431 votes, defeating the Home Rule candidate, yet falling well behind the UIL's candidate, who polled 1,424 votes. Connolly was still upbeat about the ISRP's 800 votes:

> These votes were cast for no milk-and-water, ratepaying, ambiguous 'Labour' candidates, but for the candidates of a party which in the very stress and storm of the fight instructed its standard bearers to refuse to sign the pledge of the compromising Labour Electoral body, and to stand or fall by the full spirit and meaning of its revolutionary policy. These 800 votes were cast for Socialism in spite of a campaign of calumny unequalled in its infamy, in spite of the fact that the solemn terrors of religion were invoked on behalf of the capitalist candidates, in spite of the most shameless violation by our opponents of the spirit of the Corrupt Practices' Act, and despite the boycott of the press.[25]

Despite its relative success, the ISRP failed to have any of its candidates elected, so the high point of its electoral efforts was still not good enough for it to make any breakthrough.

In 1903 the party stood two candidates. Thomas Lyng had to step in at the last moment after the original ISRP candidate, William McLoughlin, had to drop out because of problems with registration. Lyng received a paltry 102 votes in the North City Ward, the worst result so far for the party in that particular ward. Connolly witnessed his own vote in the Wood Quay Ward falling by almost 173 on the previous year. He had not been able to start campaigning until a few short weeks before polling day because he had been on a speaking tour of the United States. Yet even with this continued failure the elections did provide the party's spokesman with opportunities to make passionate addresses at public meetings. Some of Connolly's most famous speeches and writings come from this period. His speeches combined historical information with some wonderful rabble-rousing.

This, from his address to the workers of the Wood Quay Ward in 1903, gives just a flavour of the type of rhetoric he employed.

> When the workers come into the world we find that we are outcasts in the world. The land on which we must live is the property of a class who are the descendants of men who stole the land from our forefathers, and we who are workers, are, whether in town or country, compelled to pay for permission to live on the earth; the houses, shops, factories, etc., which were built by the labour of our fathers at wages that simply kept them alive are now owned by a class which never contributed an ounce of sweat to their erecting, but whose members will continue to draw rent and profit from them while the system lasts. As a result of this the worker in order to live must sell himself into the service of a master – he must sell to that master the liberty to coin into profit the physical and mental energies ... If you are a worker your interests should compel you to vote for me, if you are a decent citizen, whether worker or master, you should vote for me; if you are an enemy of freedom, a tyrant, or the tool of a tyrant, you will vote against me.[26]

Even with these great speeches Connolly was unsuccessful in his attempt to win a seat. Despite the partial success in 1902, the elections in 1903 saw the party's already small vote drop even further. This drained the morale of the party, as the other parties, which were larger and more influential, and had much more experience in the ways of electoral work (particularly the Home Rule Party) at the national level, increased their power on the local government scene. The constant failure at the polls and the party's inability to come up with any other strategy to forward the cause of socialism in Ireland were among the central reasons for the ISRP's eventual failure.

Although there were subjective reasons for the electoral failure of the ISRP, these were in the end minor difficulties. In truth the Dublin proletariat was too small and atomised, and lacked the class consciousness or the political sophistication, to adhere to the radical programme of socialist policies advocated by the ISRP. If the party had had one candidate successfully elected, as it came close to doing in 1902, this would have provided it with a significant foothold in local electoral politics, from which it could have built a power base. Lack of success bred disillusionment and eventually a huge drop in morale among the party membership. The party, and especially Connolly, was overly optimistic about its electoral strategy and the reality of failure led to huge problems within the organisation. Yet while the party suffered electoral defeat at the local level in Ireland, it was successful in participating fully in the international socialist scene.

ISRP ELECTION RESULTS 1899–1903

North Dock Ward Council Elections, January 1899	
Fleming (LEA) E	732
Harrington (HR) E	723
Holohan (Ind) E	646
Bergin (Tory) E	613
McCabe	592
E. Stewart (ISRP)	448

North Dock Ward Council Elections, January 1900	
Harrington (HR) E	N/A
Holohan (Ind) E	N/A
M. Lyng (ISRP)	N/A

North City Ward Council Elections, January 1901	
P. White (Tory) E	500
J. Allen (HR) E	411
W. McLoughlin (ISRP)	314

North City Ward Alderman Election, January 1902	
Hennessy (HR) E	751
E. Stewart (ISRP)	267

North City Ward Council Election, January 1902	
P. White MP (HR) E	536
W. McLoughlin (ISRP)	371
J. Allen (HR)	160

Wood Quay Ward Council Elections, January 1902	
P.J. McCall (HR) E	1,424
J. Connolly (ISRP)	431
W.H. Beardwood (HR)	191

North City Ward Council Elections, January 1903	
Irwin (Tory) E	736
Parkinson (UIL)	431
T. Lyng (ISRP)	102

Wood Quay Ward Council Elections, January 1903.	
Fanagan (UIL) E	763
Dodd (HR)	258
J. Connolly (ISRP)	243

E: Elected

Sources: *Workers' Republic*, ISRP Party Minutes, *Evening Herald*

The political vision of the ISRP was a global one and, although it had a particular interest in the 'national question' in Ireland its politics were extremely internationalist. The *Workers' Republic* carried a large number of international news items and the party campaigned over events occurring in foreign lands, such as the Boer War. The party had subscriptions to various foreign left-wing journals and these were avidly read by members. The party saw itself as part of the international socialist family. Commune Day, 18 March, was one of the major celebrations of the year, a hall would be booked and after a fiery speech, usually given by Connolly, party members would launch into a string of revolutionary songs, chief among them that global hymn of international socialism, the 'Internationale'. (Left-wing groups across the planet marked Commune Day in recognition of the period in 1871 when, in the wake of the Franco-Prussian War, the workers of Paris seized control of the city, before being defeated by government forces. The Commune withstood the attacks of the Versailles army from 18 March until 21 May 1871, when it was crushed, with 30,000 Communards dying in the bloodshed. Karl Marx himself saw the event as a watershed in the history of the socialist movement: the first attempt by organised workers to create their own state.[27])

After the famous German socialist Wilhelm Liebknecht, a leading member of the SPD, the largest socialist party in Europe, died in August 1900, he was recognised as one of the most prominent members of 'our' party by William Bradshaw in the pages of the *Workers' Republic*. The Dublin branch of the ISRP passed a resolution on the death of Liebknecht expressing a sense of its loss of this major figure of the international socialist movement.

> Resolved that we place on record our profound grief at the death of our illustrious comrade, Wilhelm Liebknecht, whose untiring and brilliant advocacy of the peoples' cause, has made his name known and revered wherever the militant proletariat are battling for their rights.[28]

The ISRP was a member of the Second International, which, as we have seen, was the organisational expression of the worldwide socialist movement.[29] The First International had been formed by Marx and his followers in 1864, but had been disbanded in 1876, five years after the defeat of the Commune.

The Second International, which was in contrast to the First (revolutionary and centralised) was in fact a loose association of national socialist parties of all varieties. The International was inaugurated at the International Socialist Congress in Paris in 1889. At subsequent congresses, in Brussels (1891), Zurich (1893), London (1896), Paris (1900) and Amsterdam (1904) this new International rested on strong national parties. It was the German Social Democratic Party (SPD) that dominated the International, being by far the largest organisation within it. Karl Kautsky, a leading member of the SPD, was widely seen as the principal ideologue of the International. Kautsky was often referred to by socialists at the time as the 'Pope of Marxism'. However, the International held within it socialists of various other hues, such as the Polish socialist Rosa Luxemburg, also a leading member of the SPD; Vladimir Ilyich Lenin, the Russian revolutionary and future leader of the October Revolution, and Antonio Gramsci, the Italian socialist theorist. The ISRP stood on the left of the International alongside such leading lights of the left wing of the European socialist movement. Throughout its existence the Second International witnessed some disagreements among parties regarding which road should be followed to attain socialism – essentially, whether to take the parliamentary route or a more radical revolutionary road – but this debate did not crystallise into views expressed by coherent camps for a number of decades. Around 1900 the orthodoxy of the International declared that winning a majority of seats in a parliament was the most effective way of achieving socialism.

Edward Stewart, Mark Derring and Dan O'Brien travelled as delegates representing the ISRP to the International Socialist Congress in Paris in 1900.[30] It seems that they were expected to pay their own expenses, so Paris was to be a bit of a holiday as well as an important political experience for the three young comrades from Ireland. This was the only one of the Second International's conferences to which the ISRP sent delegates. The cost of travel was too much to bear for the ISRP and anyway the next conference, in Amsterdam in 1904, was held during the final months of the ISRP's existence. According to the official report given by the delegates on their return from Paris, two of the three delegates, Derring and O'Brien, were formal representatives of the ISRP, while Stewart travelled to France representing an 'affiliated organisation, the Fintan Lalor Club, Cork'. This 'club', such as it was, was in fact nothing more than a front organisation for the ISRP. Stewart himself was from

Dublin rather than Cork and had little actual involvement with the party in Cork.

Connolly did not travel to Paris for financial reasons – in effect he could not afford the fares – although it does seem strange that the party did not collectively raise the required amount of funds to send their major thinker to the conference. Mark Derring's inclusion is almost as intriguing as Connolly's exclusion. Derring was not a major figure in the party and, although he had joined the organisation in the early months of its existence, he never held any of its senior posts. There is little doubt that Stewart and Dan O'Brien were the 'senior' members of the delegation. If Connolly had gone he would have rubbed shoulders with some of the major figures in the world of socialism and he was undoubtedly the only member of the ISRP who could have held his own in the major theoretical debates that took place at the conference. His exclusion from the delegation is both strange and a little disappointing for anyone who would have liked to see how Connolly might have intervened on the floor of the conference.

The Second International was the first international body to recognise Ireland as a nation separate from Great Britain, a fact that even impressed many of the advanced nationalists back in Ireland. This situation had not come about without some pressure being applied by the Irish delegation on the International Executive. When the International convened Henry Hyndman, the leading member of the British delegation, wanted the British and Irish delegates to sit together and divide the votes between both delegations. (Hyndman, one of the founding members of the British Socialist Democratic Federation (SDF), was the major theorist in that organisation and the young Connolly had studied much of his work in the early years of his own development as a socialist.) However, according to William O'Brien, the Irish delegates threatened to return home if they were not recognised by the Second International as separate representatives from Ireland. It seems that this course of action had been agreed with Connolly before the delegation departed for Paris.[31] In the end the ISRP's wishes were granted and the Irish delegates went on to vote as a separate grouping. In one centrally important vote it opposed the stand taken by the British delegation. Thus the ISRP's delegates expressed their independence in a concrete way.

This 'independence' was a major breakthrough for the ISRP. According to Dan O'Brien, writing after his return to Dublin, the 'mix-up' with the British delegation resulted from an oversight of 'some sort on the part of the Secretary of the Congress', who had not forwarded delegate cards to the ISRP before its representatives had departed from Dublin:

> As a result there was some difficulty in obtaining recognition as a distinct nationality. The error was happily rectified and we did not have to leave, as the only other course of action was to be part of the British delegation.[32]

In wider socialist history the conference is remembered more for the ideological and political row that split the International when the action taken by the French Socialists, led by Alexandre Millerand, was discussed on the floor of the conference. In 1899, Millerand had entered a coalition government with some conservative parties in France along with General Galliffet, who was notorious as the 'butcher in chief of the Paris Commune' because of his role in its defeat less than three decades before. When the coalition was formed in June 1899 another leading French socialist Jean Jaurès, hailed it as a major breakthrough for the socialist movement and something that the whole of the international socialist community could learn from. The ISRP's delegates did not agree and begged to differ with the eminent French socialist, already known to them as the founder of the newspaper *L'Humanité*.[33]

Although it was hard to foresee at the time, this split in the International was the first major skirmish in an ideological battle that irrevocably severed the international socialist community, essentially between those who wanted to reform the economic system by creating a capitalism with a 'human face' and others who still held to the orthodox Marxist view that capitalism could be destroyed only by a working-class revolution, peaceful or otherwise.

The atmosphere at the Paris conference was heady indeed, with anger and passion in the air: 'The battle-royal over Millerand raged for hours, during which the French "right" chanted "Vive la République" while the "left" of the international interrupted with "Vive la Commune".'[34] Yet, far from being overwhelmed or intimidated by the occasion the ISRP's delegation took a radical stance on the Millerand issue and voted consistently against the motion supporting the decision by the French Socialists to join the coalition government. The ISRP and the US Socialist Labour Party (SLP) were the only delegations that voted unanimously against the compromise resolution on the Millerand issue composed by the 'Pope' Karl Kautsky, which meant that the conference did not condemn Millerand for entering the coalition government, but rather criticised him for not getting official sanction from the majority of the French Socialist Party before doing so – in other words, a political cop-out.

The Millerand issue was the only one on which the Irish delegation voted against the majority. The fact that this was the most important and indeed the defining vote of the conference marks it as a significant stance taken by the ISRP's delegation, which indicated that the ISRP stood firmly to the left of the international socialist family. That such a delegation, made up of three young inexperienced socialists from a country that was very much on the periphery of the movement, took such a line against the majority of the international on a matter of political principle is a huge tribute to their independence of thought and action.

Despite this stance against the majority, the ISRP's delegation returned to Ireland with a very optimistic view of the state of the international socialist movement, as can be seen in the final paragraph of their report delivered to the ISRP in October:

> In reviewing the general scope and nature of the questions considered at the Congress and the decisions arrived at, we find unmistakable proof that the class conscious proletariat of the world see clearly along the lines of their own emancipation and are not likely to be led aside from the straight path by any pretended friendliness on the part of the dominant class.[35]

The detailed description of the decisions taken at the Paris conference in the report from the delegates led to a long discussion among the party's members. Connolly in particular had a problem with the decision taken by the International on the minimum wage, which stated that introduction through legislation was not the right path for socialists to follow. Connolly demurred, believing that legislation could be introduced to enforce the minimum wage. However, the dominant feeling within the party was that the delegates had represented both the party and the cause of labour in Ireland well.

The implications of the Millerand debate led to a reorientation in the ISRP's attitude to the SDF and British socialists in general. The SDF had voted in favour of Kautsky's motion on the Millerand issue at the Paris conference and, in the eyes of Connolly and the ISRP, had pushed itself firmly to the right of the international socialist movement. Writing three years after the Paris conference, Connolly attacked the SDF and its leader, Hyndman, who had by that time reversed his stance on the Millerand resolution:

> The Social Democratic Federation has been drugged into this matter in the most shameful fashion. At the Paris Congress their representatives were induced to vote for Millerand – the first of the intellectuals to sell out – chiefly by the representations of Quelch [another SDF delegate] and Hyndman, and against the advice and indignant remonstrance of the pioneers and veteran fighters of the Socialist movement in France. Now that all Quelch and Hyndman, & Co, said in favour of the compromise has been utterly falsified, and the most bitter denunciations of Millerand most amply justified, Hyndman joins in the cry against him, but even in doing so he shows no sign of shame for having voted to condone the treachery he now condemns.[36]

While Connolly still praised the abilities of Hyndman as an exponent of socialist economics, it was obvious that Connolly and, in turn, the ISRP had moved away from the SDF, a party that he had once been very close to, while at the same time moving closer to Daniel De Leon's SLP. The SLP sold the *Workers' Republic* in the United States, while in Ireland copies of the SLP's *Weekly Worker* were passed around among the ISRP's members from 1898 onwards. The foundation of the ISRP in 1896 had been thoroughly welcomed by the SLP, particularly in cities, such as Boston, in which there were very large groups of Irish immigrants. In a letter sent in September 1898 by the Boston branch of the SLP to the ISRP there is an almost evangelical tone to the excitement with which news of the formation of the ISRP had been received:

> Your arrival amongst us in America is timely. Your bold and brave tone will stir the blood of our Irish Americans; your clear vision will light the path of advance by clearing away the haze of intellectual sentiment; will turn the heart's emotion to the true cause of dependence and poverty.[37]

Connolly's writings seem to have been particularly favoured among the members of the SLP, accounting for that party's desire for Connolly to go on speaking tours of the United States as a guest of the party. Mary M. Johnson of the SLP was moved to write a poem after reading Connolly's pamphlet *Erin's Hope*. Her verse ended with the lines:

> With the light of conscience glowing,
> Comrades; ply your dauntless pen,
> Courage in your need bestowing,
> Erin's Hope is just such men.[38]

While the party was strengthening its ties with the SLP difficulties in the relationship between the ISRP and the British socialists were growing. The SDF was not the only organisation that had caused the ISRP to attack the actions of socialist organisations in Britain. In 1901 a *Remonstrance Addressed to English Socialists* from the 'Executive Committee of the Irish Socialist Republican Party' was aimed at James Keir Hardie and the Independent Labour Party (ILP) over their open support for the Irish Home Rule Party:

> For some time past Mr Keir Hardie MP and his colleagues on the *Labour Leader* newspaper have been assiduously instilling into the minds of the British Socialists the belief that Mr John Redmond's Home Rule party are burning with enthusiasm for labour and are favourably inclined towards Socialism. (We beg our readers in Ireland not to laugh at this; we are not exaggerating the case one whit.) Mr Keir Hardie has appeared on the platform with the Home Rule MPs at Irish gatherings, has given his most unqualified praise to them at gatherings of his own party – praise as staunch Labour men, please mark! – and in his paper, the aforesaid *Labour Leader*, he and another writer signing himself 'Marxian' have for the past few months left no stone unturned to imbue their readers with the belief that the Home Rule party are staunch democrats and socialistically inclined.[39]

The letter carries on, giving numerous examples of how the Home Rule Party had shown through its actions that it was not a friend of labour in Ireland. The ISRP comments on how John Redmond, the leader of the Home Rulers, had 'made himself notorious in Ireland by denouncing the agricultural labourers [at Rathfarnham] for forming a trade union' and on how Alderman McCabe in the North City Ward had 'earned the detestation of every trade unionist by voting in favour of giving painting contracts to non-union firms'.[40] The ISRP made it clear that it reacted to Keir Hardie's support of the Home Rulers with utter incredulity. Keir Hardie did not support the ISRP, because he believed it to be too left-wing and extreme. Like much of the British left, he had by this stage come to the belief that socialism was impossible in Ireland until Home Rule had been granted and thus everything had to be done to support the Home Rule cause. By 1901 his belief that labour politics could not grow in Ireland until after Home Rule was granted was reinforced after the fiasco of the LEA in local government.

The ISRP also clashed with the British socialist parties over their stance vis-à-vis their own government's actions during the Boer War. The ISRP made it clear that it had been somewhat disturbed in our mind by observing in the writings and speeches of some of our foreign comrades a tendency to discriminate in favour of Great Britain in all the international complications that country may be involved in.[41]

It seemed to the ISRP that the socialist organisations in Britain were falling into the trap of becoming exponents of nationalism rather than expressing a strong sense of internationalism. The rise in the support for imperialism within the Second International did indeed begin in this period and was to reach its peak in the collapse of the Second International in the face of the Great War in 1914. The growth of the reformist tendency in the International, which saw socialist parties express their own aims as essentially looking towards obtaining small reforms from the capitalist governments in their own countries, was mirrored in this rise in support for imperialist expansion and war. The ISRP fought against such pro-imperialist and pro-reformist tendencies, both within the International and at home in Ireland. It was with some exasperation that the ISRP bemoaned the lack of internationalist spirit in some of the European socialist parties, most critically the British socialist organisations:

We ask then is there no common ground upon which Socialists can agree to treat all matters of international politics – a common standpoint from which all questions of race or nationality shall be carefully excluded, and every question dealt with from the position of its effect upon the industrial development required to bring the Socialist movement to a head?[42]

Yet it was the very fact that the ISRP felt strong enough to launch a number of open ideological attacks on the SDF and the ILP in Britain that is of most fundamental significance when discussing the important role that the party played in the history of socialism in Ireland. In the policy and practice of the ISRP, Irish socialism was no longer just a geographical offshoot of the wider British movement. Irish socialists could now make up their own minds about tactics and policies, rather than just waiting to be spoonfed from Great Britain. Connolly was very much a product of the British labour movement, but, while he welcomed what he saw as advances for the socialist movement in Great Britain, he felt that the ISRP was in a better position to judge the needs and politics of the Irish working class than the British socialists in the SDF or the ILP.

Considering the size of the ISRP compared to that of the growing labour movement in Britain, these criticisms of the SDF and the ILP show the importance that Connolly and his party attached to their independence from British labour. It should be noted that the ISRP's attacks on the British socialist movements did not stem from any nationalist hatred, but from a spirit of comradely criticism between one socialist movement and another. As the ISRP made clear, it did not want its criticism of the British labour movement's views on Ireland to be seen as mere petty nationalist squabbling:

> As a matter of fact we would have criticised more often and more unreservedly than we have done the position of our SDF comrades were it not for the fact that they are English, and we had always an uncomfortable feeling that did we criticise them it would please the chauvinist Irishman, and we had no desire to flatter his narrow prejudices at the expense of Socialists, no matter how mistaken these latter were. But such considerations must yield to the greater gravity of the present circumstances.[43]

Although the ISRP and in particular Connolly approached British socialists as 'critical comrades', Connolly's views of the English in general did sometimes change during the period of the party's existence. In a clear statement of socialist internationalism Connolly could write of all creeds and nationalities as one, because a socialist is neither 'a Freethinker nor Christian, Turk nor Jew, Buddhist nor Idolator, Mahommedan nor Parsee it is only HUMAN'.[44] Yet he could later write about supposed fundamental racial differences between the Irish and the English: 'The national and racial characteristics of the English and Irish people are different, their political history and traditions are antagonistic.' Later in the same article Connolly writes: 'No Irish revolutionist worth his salt would refuse to lend a hand to the Social Democracy of England in the effort to uproot the social system of which the British Empire is the crown and apex.'[45]

The major advance in socialist thinking displayed by the ISRP was that the party believed that the working class and socialist parties in colonised nations could, and should, be actively involved in promoting the cause of socialism in their own countries. The working class of colonised countries did not have to trail behind the labour movements of major imperialist countries, or wait until they had achieved socialism in the metropolitan nations before the proletariat of the underdeveloped countries could be free. The ISRP displayed comradely fraternity with the socialist organisations in Britain while not feeling that this did not allow them space in which they could criticise the politics of those organisations. The ISRP and Connolly displayed progressive thinking when it came to this issue of socialism in colonised nations, as many in the Second International believed that colonialism could have beneficial, modernising effects on colonised countries. Most of the socialist parties in the advanced nations paid little or no attention to the working classes of colonised countries. Support for imperialism within the Second International was growing and it was to become the touchstone issue on which the International finally split.

The Paris conference in 1900 did pass a somewhat 'anti-colonial' resolution that was fully backed by the Irish delegation:

> That this organised proletariat ought to use every means in its power to fight capital's colonial expansion and to condemn the colonial policy of the bourgeoisie and to present the cruelty and injustice which are the awful results of the lust for capital in uncivilised parts of the world. [The Congress believes] that the formation of colonial socialist parties affiliated to those in the home countries [should] be encouraged.[46]

The fact that the ISRP signed up to a resolution that used such loaded language as 'uncivilised parts of the world' and 'home country' in reference to the colonised nations and the major metropolitan powers is interesting. Perhaps because the party had gained separate representation at the conference, the delegates felt that they could sign up to such a resolution without calling the independence of Ireland into question. Also, the ISRP did not agree that socialist parties formed in colonised nations should be affiliated to socialist parties in colonial powers, as the resolution states. The ISRP held its own independence from the British socialist parties as central to their work and programme.

That independence of thought and action on the international socialist scene was a mark of the ISRP. Even allowing for the close ties between the party and the SLP as outlined earlier in the chapter, the Irish party did not take kindly to any overt interference from its US comrades in the internal workings of the ISRP. In May 1902 Henry Kuhn, National Secretary of the SLP, wrote to the ISRP asking the Irish party to boycott the next meeting of the Second International to be held in Amsterdam in 1904, as a sign of opposition to the passing of the 'Kautsky resolution' at the International in Paris. Replying ever so politely the ISRP made it clear that while it would discuss the SLP's request, it still intended to send delegates to Amsterdam: 'We have submitted your circular to our branches as well as to our members in various districts. The ISRP intends to attend the next International Socialist Congress, should finances permit, and will move the repeal of the Kautsky resolution; should it not be repealed then we will reconsider the attitude to be taken up towards the Congress.'[47]

(For all the criticism that the ISRP heaped on British rule in Ireland, it is worth noting how relatively benign that rule was when compared to some of the more dictatorial governments that socialists had to deal with across Europe. As the Irish delegation themselves reported back, some of the socialist delegates from across the continent, 'particularly the Russian and Polish comrades', risked arrest and long jail sentences as they made their way to Paris for the conference. The ISRP's members faced no such problems when they freely left Dublin to make the journey to the French capital. The party was also able to organise relatively freely in Ireland, with open meetings and public gatherings. This was far removed from the underground network of socialists that the Bolsheviks had to deploy in Tsarist Russia.)

A growing number of socialists from parties in metropolitan countries had begun to argue that socialists should condemn the excesses of colonialism, but that it should not be opposed altogether. They believed that colonialism contained progressive features, in that it industrialised 'backward' nations and helped to create a proletariat in such countries. This growing ambivalence about colonialism could be traced to the stance taken by the ILP and SDF on the Boer War, but it found its terrible climax in 1914, when the SPD voted in favour of war credits in the German Parliament, in effect helping to launch the imperialist First World War.

The ISRP came out completely against imperialism and argued that the working class of a colonised nation such as Ireland could be the agent of its own liberation. In this the ISRP was well ahead of much of the international socialist movement. Indeed, it was to be a number of decades, taking in the many wars of national liberation in former colonised countries in the twentieth century, before socialists truly began to develop a more comprehensive philosophy and organised programme dealing with the fight for a socialist society in under-developed and colonised countries.

NOTES

1. See John Muldoon and George McSweeney, *A Guide to the Elections of County and Rural District Councillors in Ireland* (Dublin: Easons & Son, 1902).

2. Priscilla Metscher, *James Connolly and the Reconqest of Ireland* (Minnesota: Marxist Educational Press/Nature, Society, and Thought, 2002), p. 49.
3. *Workers' Republic (WR)*, Vol. 4, No. 30, Oct. 1901.
4. ISRP Programme: see Appendix One.
5. *WR*, Vol. 4, No. 33, Jan. 1902.
6. *WR*, Vol. 1, No. 11, 22 Oct. 1898.
7. Minutes, 24 Oct. 1898, in Minutes of the Irish Socialist Republican Party, 1898–1904, MS 16264–67, O'Brien Collection, National Library of Ireland (NLI).
8. Minutes, 8 Jan. 1899.
9. Austen Morgan, *Political Biography of James Connolly* (Manchester: Manchester University Press, 1988), p. 40.
10. William O'Brien, *Forth the Banners Go* (Dublin: Three Candles, 1969), p. 31.
11. *WR*, Vol. 4, No. 33, March 1902.
12. F.S.L. Lyons, *Ireland Since the Famine* (London: Fontana Press, 1985), pp. 216–60.
13. C. Desmond Greaves, *The Life and Times of Connolly* (London: Lawrence & Wishart, 1971), p. 84.
14. *WR*, Vol. 2, No. 8, 15 July 1899.
15. *WR*, Vol. 2, No. 22, 4 Nov. 1899.
16. *WR*, Vol. 2, No. 27, 30 Dec. 1899.
17. *WR*, Vol. 2, No. 28, 30 Dec. 1899.
18. Minutes, 20 Dec. 1899.
19. *WR*, Vol. 2, No. 30, 10 Feb. 1900.
20. *WR*, Vol. 2, No. 8, 15 July 1899.
21. The 'Richardson debate' is recorded in forensic detail in Minutes, 23 Dec. 1900.
22. O'Brien, *Forth the Banners Go*, p. 35.
23. Mary Daly, *Dublin the Deposed Capital: A Social and Economic History 1860–1914* (Cork: Cork University Press, 1984), pp. 218–19.
24. O'Brien, *Forth the Banners Go*, p. 33.
25. *WR*, Vol. 4, No. 33, March 1902. In this election Connolly also tried to win over the votes of the small Jewish community living in the Wood Quay Ward with the party publishing an election leaflet in Hebrew. See *ISRP Election Manifesto in Hebrew* (Dublin, ISRP, 1902) (NLI) ILB 300, p. 11 (Item 80–81). Also in the months prior to the January 1902 election the party thought about standing Con O'Lyhane in an electoral ward in Cork. However, it was decided that the Cork organisation was too weak to run an effective campaign. Letter, Con O'Lyhane to James Connolly, 27 March 1901, William O'Brien MS (NLI) 15,700 (i).
26. See Appendix Two.
27. Karl Marx, *The Civil War in France*, in Laurence H. Simon (ed.), *Karl Marx: Selected Writings* (Cambridge: Hackett Publishing Company, 1994).
28. *WR*, Vol. 3, No. 2, 18 Aug. 1900.
29. James Joll, *The Second International* (London: Weidenfield & Nicolson, 1955).
30. Historians have sent different ISRP members over to the conference, sometimes including Connolly: see Richard Michael Fox, *James Connolly:*

The Forerunner (Tralee: Kingdom Press, 1966), p. 51. Morgan, *James Connolly*, p. 41; Greaves, *Life and Times*, p. 127; and Samuel Levenson, *James Connolly: Socialist Patriot and Martyr* (London: Quartet, 1977), p. 70, have all sent Tom Lyng and Edward Stewart as the sole representatives of the ISRP to Paris. Morgan does allow for a third unnamed delegate representing the Fintan Lalor Club. However, according to O'Brien, *Go Forth the Banners*, p. 27 and the report given by the delegates in the party Minutes on 16 October 1900, Edward Stewart, Mark Deering and Dan O'Brien were the delegates who went. See also Daniel O'Brien's voting card used at the Paris International, William O'Brien manuscript (NLI) 20, 762.

31. O'Brien, *Forth the Banners Go*, p. 27.
32. Minutes, 16 Oct. 1900.
33. Greaves, *Life and Times*, pp. 126–8, Tony Cliff, *Rosa Luxemburg* (London: Bookmarks, 1986), pp. 29–31.
34. Greaves, *Life and Times*, p. 126.
35. Minutes, 16 Oct. 1900.
36. *WR*, Vol. 5, No. 9, April 1903.
37. *WR*, Vol. 1, No. 7, 24 Sept. 1898. William O'Brien noticed the closeness between the ISRP and SLP right after he joined. 'When I joined the ISRP in June 1899 I found the members very interested in the affairs of the SLP of the USA.' William O'Brien MS (NLI) 15, 674 Folder (4).
38. James Connolly, *Erin's Hope* (Dublin: *Workers' Republic* Pamphlet Series, March 1897).
39. *WR*, Vol. 4, No. 30, Oct. 1901.
40. Ibid.
41. *WR*, Vol. 2, No. 22, 4 Nov. 1899.
42. Ibid.
43. Ibid.
44. James Connolly *The New Evangel* (Dublin: New Books, 1972), p. 31.
45. James Connolly *The New Evangel and Erin's Hope: The End and The Means* (Dublin: New Island Books, 1972), p. 20.
46. Minutes, 16 Oct. 1900.
47. Letter, Mark Derring (ISRP) to Henry Kuhn (SLP) 9 July 1902. William O'Brien MS (NLI) 15, 704 (2).

CHAPTER FOUR

The ISRP on the Issues

The Protestant loyalist working class, living and working principally in the major towns of the northeastern counties in Ireland, was notable by its relative absence from the pages of the *Workers' Republic* and the general written propaganda produced by the ISRP. The issues relating to that class's religious and political allegiances were not dealt with in any systematic way by the ISRP during the period from 1896 to 1904. There were a number of reasons for this apparent oversight. The party never had a strong foothold in Belfast or any other of the major towns of the northeastern counties. (This was not something unique in itself: the party found it difficult to build any sort of support base outside of Dublin.) An attempt to form a Belfast branch of the party in 1898 foundered after a few short months. The ISRP in Belfast attracted the unwanted negative attention of loyalists and Orange Order members, but the party also failed to win the allegiance of the small number of already active Protestant and Catholic socialists in the city. Indeed, those in the Belfast socialist milieu viewed the ISRP with some suspicion. The socialists gathered around the Belfast Socialist Society seem to have regarded the philosophy of the ISRP as originating more from Irish nationalism than from international socialism. The Belfast socialists held a rather abstract view of internationalism, believing that any talk of the 'national question' in Ireland was little more than a distraction from the 'real' class issues. They believed that any potential unity between Catholic and Protestant workers along class lines would be jeopardised by any discussion of issues relating to Irish sovereignty and independence from the British Empire. The *Workers' Republic*, which was sold in Belfast, was accordingly met with some hostility from the Belfast socialists. Robert Lynd, who had been a member of the Belfast Socialist Society in 1898, reminisced two decades later:

> The first that I ever heard of him [Connolly] was when, as a student in Belfast, I belonged to a small socialist society, which met in a dusty upper room illuminated by candle sticks in empty gin bottles. One of the members used to bring copies of Connolly's paper, the *Workers' Republic*, to sell at our meetings. But most of us, I think, were indifferent to what we regarded as sentimental Nationalism. We rejected almost unanimously a proposal to adopt as our colours orange and green, and as our crest the clasped hands of the United Irishmen. We were doctrinaire Internationalists in those days and scarcely realised, as many of us do now, that Imperialism equally with capitalism means the exploitation of the weak by the strong. Socialism seemed to us like a creed for the world, while we regarded Nationalism as a merely noisy indulgence in flags and bands not different in kind from the patriotism of London stockbrokers. Connolly's lesson to Ireland was the unity of the Nationalist and Socialist ideals. Socialism with him was not a means towards a vast cosmopolitan commonness. It was a means towards a richer individual life both for human beings and for nations. True internationalist, he saw and invoked a brotherhood of equal nations as well as a brotherhood of equal citizens.[1]

The ISRP's difficulties in attempting to build socialism in Belfast in 1898 could already have been foreseen through the actions of the British ILP and SDF the decade before. Both organisations had attracted huge numbers, who attended public meetings in Belfast to hear Keir Hardie and others preach from the bible of socialism, but large and organised mobs of loyalists literally beat the socialists off the streets of Belfast.[2] Organised loyalist intimidation was a constant reaction to any attempt to build socialism within the Protestant working class in the northeastern towns. Loyalist leaders obviously feared class solidarity between Catholic and Protestant workers gaining any foothold, and thus threatening the hold of loyalism over the Protestant proletariat. Undoubtedly, conservative leaders in the Catholic 'nationalist' community' also feared the potential of socialism to undermine their power base.

The attempts made by the ISRP to build in Belfast involved little actual input from Connolly and the rest of the Dublin leadership. Connolly had too much on his plate in trying to get the Dublin branch off the ground, but his involvement with the Belfast branch still seems rather limp. He spent more time visiting the Cork branch than he did the few Belfast-based members of the party. Yet as history has shown, the lack of a coherent, coordinated socialist party building in Belfast was not the only source of failure in constructing a non-sectarian left in the city. The ISRP was not the only left-wing organisation in Ireland that failed to build solid organisational linkages between Protestant and Catholic workers in Ulster.

The question nonetheless arises whether the programme and vision of the ISRP could have ever been successful in building support among loyalist workers, even without physical intimidation or loyalist propaganda. Austen Morgan believes that Connolly's and the party's tactics towards the northeastern proletariat were deeply flawed from the start:

> Connolly imported a British conception of socialist strategy which he failed to apply to an agrarian and nationalist Ireland, where Catholic politics avoided the minority problem of the Ulster Protestants.[3]

Morgan is right to suggest that the party tended to ape the problems of more traditional Catholic nationalist politics with its lack of engagement with or understanding of the loyalist proletariat. But there is little doubt that the party's ultimate political vision was of a secular workers' republic in Ireland as enshrined in the party's programme of 1896, a republic that would have respected the religious rights of all its citizens, whether Protestant or Catholic. As already noted, the democratic control of the national schools was of central importance as part of the party's minimum programme. This proposal was an attempt to break the ideological and practical control that the major churches had over children's education. However, the ISRP and Connolly's failure to publicly 'face down' the Catholic Church led some to question whether an independent Ireland (even a workers' republic) would not have seen the Catholic Church still having major influence, with the Protestant minority frozen out.

Discussions regarding religion within the ISRP were strictly forbidden, so no major debate dealing with the material foundations of religious belief ever took place within the party. Connolly feared that the ISRP could have been viewed as irreligious by the Irish working class, thus making it more difficult for the party to build in a strongly religious country where the Catholic clergy had so much influence.

Connolly's stance on this ban on discussion of religious matters can be seen in its most extreme form in an incident that occurred in March 1899. Edward Stewart, the ISRP's unsuccessful candidate in the election two months before, wrote an article for the British socialist paper *Justice* regarding the election in the North Dock Ward,[4] which included this sentence: 'Though the Church cursed, the politicians swore and the pure and simplers acted treacherously, we succeeded in polling four hundred and fifty votes.'[5] At the next business meeting of the ISRP Connolly highlighted the article and criticised Stewart sharply for the use of the phrase the 'Church cursed'. Stewart argued in his own defence that the article was not meant to be taken as a comprehensive account of the election, rather as a personal view of the poll. He also claimed that he did not know that the piece was to be published, although this seems rather unlikely, and pointed out that the party had indeed been criticised from the pulpit during the election. Notwithstanding Stewart's defence, Connolly moved a motion of censure on him for the use of the phrase in the article, and this motion was passed. Connolly's reaction to just one phrase in a short article in a foreign journal clearly shows how seriously he took the ban on religious discussion.

Despite the attempts by the ISRP to stay away from matters religious, the party was still criticised from the pulpit. Connolly attempted to deal with these clerical attacks by using quotations from religious leaders and items of Church history to try to prove that the teachings of Christianity were not in opposition to the tenets of socialism.[6] While Connolly himself died a Catholic, his own personal faith, such as it was, was not all that strong and his public stance as a Catholic was more tactical than anything else.[7]

The majority of the party's members welcomed the reluctance of the ISRP to produce propaganda attacking the political and ideological role played by the Catholic Church in supporting the economic status quo in Ireland, and those who did raise religious issues at meetings were severely reprimanded. The party, chiefly through the writings of Connolly, made it clear that it did not believe socialism to be in any fundamental way an opponent of organised religion. Despite this reluctance to openly criticise, or even to discuss, the teachings and beliefs of the Catholic Church, Connolly was no fan of any brand of 'Christian socialism', believing that the two ideologies should remain separate. An early resolution to have the party called the 'Christian Socialist Party' was defeated, with Connolly being one of the chief opponents.[8] Connolly had a general reluctance to discuss moral or sexual issues in a socialist context. He described socialists who wrote about sexual relations or moral problems in socialist journals as 'faddists' and he believed that socialism was centrally an economic theory.

Yet not all of the organisation's members agreed with his attitude to organised religion. Con O'Lyhane, the ISRP's leader in Cork, and one of the most intelligent and active of the party' members, was one such dissident. The branch in Cork had a short and difficult life between 1897 and 1902, and much of the difficulty was caused by the local clergy, who preached against the evils of socialism and particularly the ISRP from the pulpits of Cork's Catholic churches.[9] In 1902 O'Lyhane had to flee Cork after he was dismissed from his job as a consequence of a bishop's letter read from the pulpit condemning socialism. O'Lyhane believed that both Connolly's stance and the party's general attitude towards the Church were exposing the ISRP to unanswered clerical attacks. Indeed, O'Lyhane fell out with Connolly, snidely calling the party's Secretary 'Catholic Connolly'. However, despite the constant religious harassment, at various times O'Lyhane was confident that the party could grow in the 'rebel city':

> The R.C. Bishop has fulminated against us, and the *Cork Examiner* has devoted its leading article in last Monday's issue to our propaganda. Please get out the next issue as soon as you can, and send on 20 dozen copies to go on with. If we can successfully steer our bark over the present wave of clerical opposition our party is made in Cork.[10]

In the end O'Lyhane and the ISRP were not able to overcome the clerical opposition to the party in Cork. O'Lyhane eventually left the party, bitterly believing that he and his branch had not received enough support from his Dublin comrades, and in particular Connolly, when it came to the attacks from the Church.

The Cork branch's difficulties with the local clergy and Connolly's reaction serve to highlight the rather peculiar relationship that Connolly the convinced socialist was to have with Catholicism for the rest of his life. Connolly's attitude to the Catholic Church shaped the wider party, and it was an attitude marked by an extreme defensiveness. The ISRP was petrified of provoking the wrath of the Catholic Church in case the pulpit would be used to turn the hearts and heads of the Irish proletariat even further away from socialism. Ironically, despite the attempts by the ISRP to remain neutral with regard to the church's teachings, the party was still condemned from the pulpit for its supposed irreligious beliefs. One can understand O'Lyhane's impatience with Connolly's stance on Catholic matters: while the ISRP's man in Cork was being hounded by the local clergy,

the ISRP in Dublin provided little in the way of support, encouragement or defence.

The ban on religious discussion within the party was also a rather
ham-fisted measure, instigated by Connolly to prevent any
expression of 'irreligious' beliefs within the ISRP. This tactic of trying
to ignore religion was born out of an understandable reaction to
working within a proletariat unused to the philosophy of socialism
and still heavily influenced by Catholic teachings. This may have
been understandable, but in the end it proved futile.

The ISRP seems not to have had a Marxist understanding of
religion. Marx famously declared religion the 'opium of the people'.
However, rather than just seeing religion as a source of solace for
people in an uncaring world, or as principally a reactionary ideology
preventing them from trying to change the world, because it held out
hope for a paradise in the afterlife, Marx actually formulated a much
more sympathetic and sophisticated view of religious belief. Marx
believed that religion was a product of man's alienation under the
economic system. Those who laboured under capitalism had no
control over the work that they undertook, work that was ruled by
capitalists, nor did the workers have a say in what to do with the
products of their labour. Workers were therefore alienated from their
own labour process, and thus also from the economic and social
system. God was created by human beings as an ideal ideological
representation of unalienated and complete humanity, a humanity
that workers living and working under the capitalist mode of
production could not achieve. Therefore socialists could not
ideologically defeat workers' belief in religion just by using
rationalist arguments against belief in the divine (i.e. there is no
material evidence for the existence of a god): the objective economic
conditions that created alienation under capitalism would have to be
changed before idealistic belief in God could dissolve away.[11]

The ISRP was extremely unsure of its ideological footing in relation
to the Catholic Church and thus ceded huge ground to the bishops.
This retreat was a product of defensiveness on the issue, rather than
any real respect for the institution of the Church itself. However, it is
understandable that many socialists outside and on the fringes of the
organisation viewed this as the party refusing to take on the Catholic
Church. This led some to believe that the ISRP had some sort of
conservative Catholic leanings.

Despite these problems the ISRP remained deeply anti-sectarian
and, in theory at least, believed that the Catholic and Protestant

working class could be united around the call for socialism. Connolly himself finished the final chapter of his *Labour in Irish History* with the optimistic hope that socialism could lead to unity on class lines:

> In their movement the North and South will again clasp hands, again will it be demonstrated, as in '98, that the pressure of a common exploitation can make enthusiastic rebels out of a Protestant working class; earnest champions of civil and religious liberty out of Catholics, and out of both a united social democracy.[12]

LAND

The ISRP throughout its existence was an overwhelmingly urban organisation. Almost all of its agitation took place in the main towns and little or no work was carried out in the countryside. Connolly did travel through the southern counties of Kerry and Cork during a famine in 1897, and composed a proclamation calling on the peasants to learn from the mistakes of the Great Famine of the 1840s and seize food that was to be exported. He also reported for the American SLP's paper the *Weekly Worker* on the food crisis facing the Irish peasantry. Considering the significant Irish immigrant readership that paper had, it can be taken for certain that his reports would have been avidly read by people who could remember or had already been told about the Great Famine. Yet this was a rare journey into the rural counties for a member of the ISRP. Ireland was an overwhelmingly rural society, the vast majority of the population being based in the countryside: thus day-to-day existence in the ISRP did not come into contact with a substantial section of the Irish people.

The ISRP was very much like the rest of the socialist parties in the Second International when it came to policy positions regarding the peasantry and the land question. Socialist ideology and practice were principally focused on the urban working class. Socialism held that it was the proletariat that was to be the agency for revolutionary change in society, as it was the only class with the economic strength and political reason to threaten the workings of the capitalist system. While the ISRP was fully aware of the huge size of the rural population in Ireland relative to the small urban proletariat, as well as the importance of the issue of land ownership, it did not believe that these were absolute barriers to socialist development in Ireland: 'We quite appreciate the fact that peasants proprietary [private ownership of land] is somewhat of a hindrance to the spread of Socialist ideas, but an effective bulwark for capitalism it decidedly is not.'[13]

The ISRP did have a very distinct and clear view of how the land question was to be resolved. In the party's programme of 1896 the land question features prominently, with the third point calling for the 'establishment at public expense of rural depots for the most improved agricultural machinery, to be lent out to the agricultural population at a rent covering cost and management alone'.[14] The ISRP believed that agriculture in Ireland was lagging well behind that of other countries such as the United States, where large farms with the best machinery had now massively increased their output. The ISRP argued that the main thing to be done was to try to modernise the methods used by the peasants and farmers as quickly as possible.

In 1899 the third point of the ISRP's programme became a source of disagreement between the two major socialist parties in the United States, the SLP and the Social Democrat Party. The SLP was radical while the Social Democrats were relatively more mainstream, seeking to reform capitalism rather than to overthrow it through revolution. The Social Democrats used the stated policy of the ISRP on rural depots as an example of a policy intended to provide protection for small farmers. The Social Democrats had made the protection of the small farmers a central plank of their rural policies, while the SLP argued that land nationalisation should be the aim of any future socialist government in the United States. As noted before, the ISRP was very close politically to the SLP and, as was to be expected, Connolly intervened in the debate on the side of Daniel De Leon's organisation. According to Connolly, the third point of the ISRP's programme was a demand made specifically in the Irish context. Irish agriculture lagged so far behind its international competitors that an effort must be made forthwith to try to modernise it. In contrast, agriculture was at the forefront of US modernisation and thus did not need such initiatives:

> The Farmers' Demands of the Social Democrats of America are demands which aim at the perpetuation of the system of petty farming by legislation to protect it from the effects of the competition of farms managed on those lines most nearly approximating to the Socialist form of industry, viz., the lines of centralised capital, and agricultural armies. American agriculture, as such, is not in any danger as a source of support for the agriculturist. His status may be endangered, not his existence. The Farmers' Demands of the Socialist Republican Party of Ireland are

demands which aim at preserving Agriculture in Ireland from being annihilated as a native industry by the competition of foreign agriculturists. Irish agriculturists are not threatened with absorption, but with extinction and enforced exile.[15]

In essence the ISRP's demand for the introduction of rural depots was very much a 'minimum' policy intended to prevent the continued emigration of Irish people from rural areas, and also to prevent further famine and absolute poverty in the rural counties. Connolly held that any major capitalist industrialisation in Ireland was an impossibility: a socialist Ireland would remain a predominantly agricultural country that would trade goods with more industrialised nations. The desire for the rapid modernisation of Irish agriculture can be seen against this theoretical background. The US Social Democrats wanted to protect smallholders; the ISRP wanted to protect the very future of Irish agriculture:

> ...the American Farmers' Demands are in the interest of one particular form of agricultural enterprise, as against another; the Irish Demands are directed towards rescuing agriculture itself, and teaching the agriculturist to look to national co-operation as the factor he should count upon for help in his struggle to remain in the country of his birth. Given American conditions in Ireland, the Irish Socialists would wipe their Farmers' Demands from off their programme, but in Ireland as it is with the rags of a medieval system of land tenure still choking our life and cramping our industry, with perennial famine destroying our people, with our population dwindling away by emigrations, we consider it right to point out, even if unheeded, that it is the duty of the State to undertake the functions of manufacture and custodian of all implements required for the one important industry of the country – agriculture. This is all we demand in that nature:– Establishment at public expense of rural depots for the most improved agricultural machinery, to be lent out to the agricultural population at a rent covering cost and management alone. It is not a sectional demand, but is the outcome of a national exigency.[16]

Irish agriculture in the 1890s was in a very poor economic state and, with little growth in manufacturing in the southern part of the country, the prospects for the whole of the Irish economy were not good. While the ISRP did see some radical aspects to the 'Land War' that spread across Ireland in the final two decades of the nineteenth century, as Catholic Irish farmers sought to win land ownership, it is useful to note that by the mid-1890s many conservative politicians also wished to see a settlement to the land question in Ireland. This desire arose, not from a concern over the inequities inherent in the remnants of the landlord system, but from a wish to see the issue dealt with as part of a 'constructive unionist' programme. If a new class of Irish landowners could be satisfied with a land settlement, a fundamental component of the continued disorder in Ireland would disappear. Indeed, a contented rural class of landowners in Ireland could form the basis of a new and rather conservative class that could become a bulwark against any radical politics emanating from the urban areas of Ireland.

Because of their socialist politics Connolly and the ISRP clearly understood the contradictory nature of the land question. While the peasants were fighting for land ownership they would remain radical, but once land had been won the rural class would tend to become one of the most conservative sections of society. Connolly knew his history well enough to be able to be draw from the example of France and other countries, where the once revolutionary peasants quickly fell back into a more conservative outlook when they had gained their land. Despite this awareness, Connolly did not believe that the existence of a large peasant population in Ireland presented a barrier to socialism that the ISRP and the Irish working class could not overcome:

> Two of the countries named as possessing a peasant proprietary, and therefore as safe from socialism, are just the two countries in which socialism is strongest, viz., France and Germany...In fact, peasant proprietary is rather belated in Ireland just now to be an effective barrier against the spread of socialist principles. We do not need to fight peasant proprietary, we only need to allow free scope for the development of capitalist enterprise in order to see the system of small farming crushed out by the competition of the great farms and scientific cultivation of America and Australia.[17]

Thus the ISRP supported the landless during the Land War, while being fully aware of the conservative settlement that would eventually result from it. Of course the ISRP's maximum programme for Irish agriculture was for land nationalisation, but that would not be on the agenda for some time because of the backwardness of the rural economy. Connolly viewed the large industrial farms already in existence in the United States in a favourable light and saw it as almost inevitable that such farms would be formed in Ireland if communal rural depots were introduced.

The actual method of achieving land nationalisation was not discussed in any detail in the writings of the ISRP, whether through the abolition of inheritance rights by decree, the creation of model nationalised farms to impress landowners with their effectiveness, or forced collectivisation. It seems that Connolly believed that the inherent logic of the need for nationalisation and communal work on the farms of Ireland would convince the peasants. Connolly argued that only full nationalisation, with extensive pooling of labour and high-class machinery, could allow Irish farmers to catch up with developments in agriculture on the international level, thus allowing them to compete on foreign markets:

> When agriculture ceases to be a private enterprise, when a free nation organises the production of its own foodstuffs as a public function, and intrusts the management of the function to the agricultural population, under popular boards of their own election, then the 'keen individualism of the Irish peasant' will find its expression in constant watchfulness over the common stock and supervision of each other's labour, and will form the best security against wastefulness, and the best incentive to honest toil. When the land is the property of the people in the fullest sense (all the people whether in town or country), then all the aids to agriculture which science supplies, but which are impossible to the poverty-stricken peasant, will be utilised by the national administrators and placed at the service of the cultivators of the soil.[18]

Yet the nature of this socialistic land settlement was never laid out in detail by the ISRP. This blind spot in the theory of the party is understandable, considering that the questions raised by the Land War had yet to be fully resolved by the various Land Acts introduced during the 1890s and the early years of the twentieth century. In the end, however, the ISRP's concern that a conservative land settlement would result in a rather weak agricultural sector falling further behind the more modern farming methods used in the United States and other nations proved prophetic. This was the basic situation in the countryside after all the Land Acts had been implemented, as an increasingly conservative class of Irish landowners presided over an agricultural system in deep crisis.

Land nationalisation, or even the third point of the ISRP's programme, never gained any significant following in the country-side, although Michael Davitt, one of the leaders of the Land League, was personally in favour of land nationalisation. Connolly believed that land nationalisation in the final analysis was fundamental to the success of any future Irish Socialist Republic and that any proprietary peasant class resulting from the Land War would in the end have to be replaced by large-scale nationalisation of land:

> To make the land of a country the property of a class is to my mind equally iniquitous, whether that class number a few hundreds or a few thousands. The land of a country belongs of right to the people of that country, and not to any particular class, not even to any single generation of the people. The private ownership of land by the landlord class is an injustice to the whole community, but the creation of a peasant proprietary would only tend to stereotype and consecrate that injustice.[19]

The class struggle in the Irish countryside was very real in the closing years of the nineteenth century, but the role that the ISRP could have played within the struggle was not all that great. The ISRP was severely restricted, since the organised urban working class comprised an extremely conservative trade union structure, with very little class struggle evident. Indeed, the conservative craft trade unions were not very supportive of the Land War and rather uninterested in the struggle for land ownership taking place in rural Ireland. Unlike during great revolutionary periods, as in Russia in 1917 or France in 1789, class warfare in the cities and the countryside did not happen concurrently in Ireland. While the class struggle was raging on the land during the existence of the ISRP, the working class in the cities was much less militant. The radical synergy that could have occurred if both country and city had been militant at the same time never materialised, and the ISRP did not have the opportunity to sink any real roots into the Irish countryside. Although Connolly had shown his deep concern for the plight of the Irish peasantry with his tour of the famine-wrecked counties in 1897, the ISRP's proposals for agricultural modernisation and eventual land nationalisation had little or no impact on the general discussions regarding the future of rural Ireland.

NATIONALISM

Connolly and other members of the ISRP were very closely involved in the milieu that surrounded the Gaelic Revival in the 1890s and early twentieth century including the Gaelic League, founded in 1893; the Gaelic Athletic Association, founded in 1884, and the output of the Irish Literary Revival, most closely focused around the Abbey Theatre in Dublin, founded in 1904. Austen Morgan has wrongly stated that during the Gaelic Revival Connolly 'tossed aside Irish cultural nationalism'.[20] In backing up this claim Morgan uses Connolly's oft-quoted remark that 'You cannot teach starving men Gaelic.'[21] Rather than interpreting the renewed interest in Irish culture as something that the ISRP should have no interest in, this remark in fact displays Connolly's priorities. Like orthodox Marxists, he believed the economic state of society to be the most important gauge of how the working class was faring. In this remark he was attacking the more bourgeois elements of the Gaelic Revival, who focused less on the starvation faced by many Irish people, in both rural and urban areas, than on their literary sensibilities and cultural education.

In fact the party was closely involved in the revival and was generally very well-disposed to many of its important figures. As we have seen, the writer Fred Ryan was close to the party and joined it for a short period. Ryan became one of the founding members of the Abbey Theatre. He lectured members of the ISRP on such erudite topics as the works of Ibsen and in a lecture entitled 'A Note on the Democratic Drama', dealt with the works of Bernard Shaw.[22] William O'Brien attended plays produced during the Literary Revival with Connolly and remembered Connolly introducing him to the republican writer Alice Milligan at one such production. O'Brien himself was at the Abbey Theatre on the first night of J.M. Synge's *The Playboy of the Western World* in 1907, which caused such a controversy in literary Ireland.[23] The party was generally supportive of the burgeoning interest in all things culturally Irish, both in Dublin and further afield. Indeed, Connolly's *Labour in Irish History*, which was written during this period, could be seen as part of the output of the Irish Literary Revival. The book attempts to uncover a hidden history of the Irish working people that had not yet been told. In doing so it emphasises the need for Irish independence and how British colonialism had determinately affected Irish society and culture since the Norman invasion.

Whether the ISRP itself was a 'nationalist' party, in the sense that, for example, Sinn Féin was a 'nationalist' party from its establishment in 1905, is a rather moot point. William O'Brien, for one, believed that the ISRP was very much a nationalist organisation 'in addition to being a socialist body was very definitely nationalist and advanced nationalist at that'.[24] This is the reminiscences of a party member many decades after its demise, while also expressing the nationalist politics that O'Brien developed in the decades after the collapse. Yet it seems that he was not the only person at the time to believe that the ISRP was very much a nationalist organisation. As already noted, the socialists in Belfast also looked on the ISRP with some suspicion, as nothing more than a nationalist organisation with a thin socialistic veneer.

Nevertheless, the attitude of the ISRP to nationalism was a complex one. First, the party drew a clear distinction between the Irish Home Rule Party and the advanced nationalists. The Home Rulers were seen as nothing more than supporters of the status quo, Irish Tories who represented the interests of the big landowners and Irish industry:

> Every succeeding year has seen the Parnellite party become more and more conservative and reactionary. Today, in direct opposition to the policy of their great leader, we find the Parnellite chiefs seeking every opportunity to hob-nob with the representatives of Irish landlordism; hailing their feeblest utterances upon a financial question as the brightest scintillations of wisdom; and not scrupling to tell at Cambridge an audience, composed of the young fledglings of English aristocracy, that the realisation of Ireland's independence was neither possible nor desirable. Followers of Parnell they are indeed, but they follow at such a respectable distance they have lost sight not only of the leader but of his principles.[25]

The advanced nationalists were viewed in a completely different light from these Home Rulers, since the ISRP saw the republicans as essentially progressive in nature. The ISRP did criticise the republicans on a number of matters such as the idolisation of the gun within the 'physical force' tradition of republicanism:

> Ireland occupies a position among the nations of the Earth unique in a great variety of its aspects, but in no one particular is this singularity more marked than in the possession of what is known as a 'physical force party' – a party, that is to say, whose members are united upon no one point, and agree upon no single principle, except upon the use of physical force as the sole means of settling the dispute between the people of this country and the governing power of Great Britain.[26]

However, in the greater scheme of things this seemed a rather minor matter, and Connolly and his party manfully tried for many years to win over the supporters of Arthur Griffith and other republicans to the politics of the ISRP.

As Kieran Allen has pointed out, Connolly's general support for the Irish republican cause originated from two principal sources.[27] First, Connolly argued in his writings that capitalism in Ireland was an inherently foreign phenomenon that came by way of the Norman invasion in the twelfth century. According to Connolly, this capitalistic ethic and practical economics began to replace the clan-based Irish communal economic system. Second, Connolly believed that major capitalist development in Ireland was impossible. In his pamphlet *Erin's Hope* he argues that the worldwide capitalist market had become glutted and that the space for any more capitalist expansion was severely limited.

> Remember all this, and then tell me how poor Ireland, exhausted and drained of her life-blood at every pore, with a population almost wholly agricultural and unused to mechanical pursuits, is to establish new factories, and where she is to find the customers to keep them going. She cannot create new markets. This world is only limited after all, and the nations of Europe are pushing their way into its remote corners so rapidly that in a few years time, at most, the entire world will have been exhausted as a market for their wares.[28]

Thus Connolly believed that Arthur Griffith's agenda of self-sufficiency, with tariff barriers to help to nurture indigenous capitalism in a free and independent Ireland, was nothing more than a dream. Connolly rather optimistically believed that the failure of capitalism to develop in Ireland would prove Griffith's thesis false and that Griffith would eventually have to adopt the ISRP's political platform. These central planks of Connolly's politics led to a problematic political orientation towards the advanced nationalist groupings. Both the assumptions that Connolly made regarding capitalism in Ireland were highly suspect. He did not believe that advanced nationalists would support capitalism in the final analysis, even if they expressed their own desire to see capitalist development as Griffith did, because in the end capitalism was a foreign import: 'Because he believed that the struggle for Irish independence led to an assault on capitalism itself, he did not recognise the extent to which even militant Republicans could contribute to capitalism's survival.'[29]

The belief that the ancient system of clans in Ireland was inherently communistic and the assertion that capitalism, with bourgeois ownership of property, resulted from foreign invasion hardly constituted a Marxist view of history. In any case Connolly believed that there could be no return to the ancient form of 'Celtic communism' and he also argued that capitalism would have developed in Ireland eventually with or without a Norman invasion. The future socialist society would be a 'reorganisation of society on the basis of a broader and more developed form of that common property which underlay the social structure of Ancient Erin'.[30] These conditions in Connolly's thesis point to the tactical nature of his writings on Irish republicanism. In no other historical context did he apply this view of the growth of capitalism. Only in the case of Ireland did he argue that capitalism is essentially a foreign import and that nationalists who embraced capitalistic forms of development were being untrue to their 'real politics'. One may assume that Connolly was tactically trying to 'Hibernicise' his socialist philosophy. Making its politics more palatable to the advanced nationalists was, after all, a constant theme in the propaganda of the ISRP, and in the pages of the *Workers' Republic* Connolly continually played down the differences between the ISRP and the advanced nationalists.

This constant attempt to build bridges, particularly with Griffith, led to some limited success when Griffith endorsed Connolly's candidature in the local elections in 1903. However, Griffith endorsed only Connolly the individual, rather than the ISRP. He never changed his belief in the need to build up capitalism in Ireland, or his strong adherence to protectionism as advanced by the German economist Friedrich List. Griffith would later be an opponent of Larkinism and was never convinced by Connolly's vision of a socialist workers' republic.[31]

The only time that Connolly changed his position somewhat regarding the advanced nationalists was after the fiasco of the 1798 commemorations, when the republicans allowed the Home Rulers to take over the organisation of the commemorations. He chided the republicans for their constant concerns to create an 'all class alliance' within the nationalist movement. He wondered what major changes the republicans would introduce in Ireland if they ever succeeded in getting rid of the British and declaring a free and independent state, as these extracts from his article 'Let Us Free Ireland' show:

> Let us free Ireland! Never mind such base, carnal thoughts as concern for work and wages, healthy homes, or lives unclouded by poverty...Let us free Ireland! The rackrenting landlord; is he not

also an Irishman, and wherefore should we hate him? Nay, let us not speak harshly of our brother – yea, even when he raises our rent... Let us free Ireland, says the patriot who won't touch Socialism. Let us all join together and cr-r-rush the br-r-rutal Saxon... Let us all join together, says he, all classes and creeds. And, says the town worker, after we have crushed the Saxon and freed Ireland, what will we do? Oh, then you can go back to your slums, same as before. Whoop it up for liberty!... With the Green Flag floating o'er us' and an ever-increasing army of unemployed workers walking about under the Green Flag, wishing they had something to eat. Same as now! Whoop it up for liberty!... Now, my friend, I also am Irish, but I'm a bit more logical. The capitalist, I say, is a parasite on industry; as useless in the present stage of our industrial development as any other parasite in the animal or vegetable world is to the life of the animal or vegetable upon which it feeds.[32]

Despite this, the ISRP continued to stick to the strongly held conviction that the republicans would eventually, almost naturally, come to be convinced by its political agenda:

Our honest and uncompromising nationalist friends may not choose to own up to the fact but they are nevertheless rapidly forced to adopt the line of action we have all along advocated as the only possible one for a revolutionary party which really means business. That line of action spells uncompromising hostility to all half way men and measures.[33]

This optimism proved to be fatal to the future of the ISRP because advanced nationalists never came to join the party in any large or even small numbers. While Connolly in later years influenced the republican movement somewhat, between 1896 and 1904 the ISRP completely failed to convince advanced nationalists of the need to adopt its political programme.

NOTES

1. Robert Lynd in his *Introduction to James Connolly, The Reconquest of Ireland* (Dublin: Transport and General Worker's Union, 1944), p. xix.
2. Fintan Lane, *The Origins of Modern Irish Socialism, 1881–1896* (Cork: Cork University Press, 1997), pp. 192–6.
3. Austen Morgan, *Political Biography of James Connolly* (Manchester: Manchester University Press, 1988), p. 45.
4. Minutes, 13 March 1899, in Minutes of the Irish Socialist Republican

Party, 1898–1904, MS 16264–67, O'Brien Collection, National Library of Ireland (NLI).

5. Minutes, 13 March 1899.
6. Kieran Allen, *The Politics of James Connolly* (London: Pluto Press, 1990), pp. 23–9.
7. W.K. Anderson, *James Connolly and the Irish Left* (Dublin: Irish Academic Press, 1994), pp. 26–7.
8. Sean Cronin, *Young Connolly* (Dublin: Repsol, 1983), p. 43.
9. Ibid., p. 59. Rather confusingly the Con O'Lyhane who wrote to Connolly about these clerical attacks on the party in Cork used different versions of his name in different periods of his political life. 'I am known here as Con Lyhane; sometimes Con O'Lyhane. The latter in Gaelic circles, where a supreme act of patriotism consists in prefixing an 'O' to a hitherto Anglicised surname, Carroll was my mother's maiden name.' Letter, Con O'Lyhane to James Connolly, 3 Feb. 1900: William O'Brien MS (NLI) 15,700 (ii). He also used the spelling Con Lehane when working in London and New York in the later years of his life.
10. Ibid., p. 63. Some of the friction between O'Lyhane and Connolly over religious issues also reached the pages of the *Workers' Republic*, if only in an extremely subtle form. In an article written by O'Lyhane under his pseudonym 'Proletarian' the Cork man strayed onto the religious issues arising from the Dreyfus Affair in France: 'But I find I have digressed and wandered into Spailpin's [Connolly's] territory – a step which he will, I am afraid, resent': *Workers' Republic* (*WR*), Vol. 2, No. 4, 26 May 1899.
11. See Karl Marx, 'Towards a Critique of Hegel's Philosophy of Right, An Introduction', in Laurence H. Simon (ed.), *Karl Marx: Selected Writings* (Cambridge: Hackett Publishing Company, 1994).
12. James Connolly, *Labour in Irish History* (London: Bookmarks, 1987), p. 167.
13. *WR*, Vol. 1, No. 3, 27 Aug. 1898.
14. ISRP Programme: see Appendix One.
15. *WR*, Vol. 2, No. 20, 21 Oct. 1899.
16. Ibid.
17. *WR*, Vol. 1, No. 3, 27 Aug. 1898.
18. Ibid.
19. James Connolly, *Erin's Hope: The End and the Means* (Dublin: New Books, 1972), pp. 13–14.
20. Morgan, *James Connolly*, p. 31.
21. *WR*, Vol. 1, No. 7, 1 Oct. 1898. Connolly also wrote: 'The chief enemy of a Celtic revival today is the crushing force of capitalism': *WR*, Vol. 1. No. 7, 1 Oct. 1898.
22. Allen, *The Politics of James Connolly*, p. 15.
23. William O'Brien, *Forth the Banners Go* (Dublin: Three Candles, 1969), p. 19.
24. Ibid., p. 8.
25. *WR*, Vol. 1, No. 8, 8 Oct. 1898.
26. *WR*, Vol. 4, No. 26, May 1901.
27. Allen, *The Politics of James Connolly*, pp. 35–7.
28. Connolly, *Erin's Hope*, p. 12.
29. Shaun Doherty, 'Will the Real James Connolly Please Stand Up',

International Socialism Journal, 80, Sept. 1998.
30. James Connolly, *Socialism and Nationalism* (Dublin: Three Candles, 1948), p. 25.
31. Padraig Yates, *Lockout Dublin 1913* (Dublin: Gill & Macmillian, 2000), pp. 132–4.
32. James Connolly, *Socialism Made Easy* (Dublin: The Plough Book Service, 1971), pp. 31–2 and *WR*, Vol. 4, No. 23, Feb. 1901.
33. *WR*, Vol. 3, No. 6, 23 June 1900.

CHAPTER FIVE

The Demise of the ISRP, 1902–04

'LIKE THE LOSS OF A CHILD'

A shallow reading of the ISRP's minutes from early 1903 might lead the historian to believe that the final months of its history show a party violently turning in on itself, in a petty and small-minded orgy of political self-abuse. The party that its members had worked so hard to create and nurture over eight years, in extremely difficult circumstances, virtually collapsed in the space of six months amid a welter of personal abuse and accusation. A bitter and long-lasting taste was to remain in the mouths of many of the participants involved in the dying days of the organisation.

Connolly compared his feeling on the death of the party to that of losing one of his children.[1] Writing to his friend John Mulray in late 1904, a year after he had left both the party and Ireland, he was still bitter as he considered the legacy left by the ISRP and the remaining socialists he left behind in Dublin. 'At any rate I regard Ireland, or at least the Socialist part of Ireland which is all I care for, as having thrown me out, and I do not wish to return like a dog to his vomit.'[2]

The surface manifestations of the terminal sickness in the party took various forms, but they reflected the more deep-seated difficulties that the organisation was facing. Personal vilification, drink, financial problems, accusations of bullying, expulsion, resignations and final implosion all in turn sucked the lifeblood from the small organisation. The final months of 1902 and the early period of 1903 saw the party take blow after blow before turning its bile in on itself.

The decline in the party's fortunes was a creeping one. Connolly felt sure enough of the future of the ISRP to write in the *Worker's Republic* in March 1902 that the party had against it 'all the organised forces of society – of a society founded upon robbery, but it had on its side a latent force stronger than them all, the material interests of the Working Class'.[3] In this piece, entitled, 'Taken Root', Connolly wrote positively about the ISRP's past and its future:

> But that little band of pioneers stuck to their work manfully, and despite all discouragements and rebuffs continued sowing the seeds of Socialist working-class revolt in the furrows of discontent ploughed by the capitalist system of society. To-day they can look back on their work with pride. Nowhere, it is true, have they yet succeeded in getting on their side that majority necessary to place the nominee of their party, the SRP, on the seats of the elected ones – that triumph is indeed not yet vouchsafed to them – but he would indeed be a very ignorant or a very presumptuous person who would essay to review the possibilities of the political situation in Dublin, and would leave this little fighting party out of his calculations.[4]

Whether this was an example of Connolly burying his head in the sand, or a flight of undue optimism, is difficult to judge.

Yet whatever Connolly's true feelings when he wrote this, his speculation about the future of the party proved to be wildly inaccurate. The party was to be teetering on the brink of disaster just twelve months after he expressed this rose-tinted view of the ISRP's chances in the local elections of January 1903.

In September 1902 Connolly flagged his news of an impending journey to the United States in the *Workers' Republic*. He was to undertake a speaking tour as a guest of Daniel De Leon's SLP and would also try and raise funds for the ISRP.[5] The influence of the SLP on a section of the Irish party's membership (in particular Connolly) was growing. The *Workers' Republic* increasingly published material from the SLP and De Leon's articles were printed prominently in the paper. As already noted, the SLP's paper, *Weekly People*, was sent over and was circulated among the ISRP's members from 1898 onwards. Relations between the two parties had been further strengthened after they had found themselves on the 'left' of the Second International during the Millerand debate in Paris in 1900. Connolly had already tried to build an SLP current in Great Britain during speaking and fund-raising visits there, and his move away from the British SDF was matched only by his closer alignment to the political programme of De Leon's organisation.

Connolly's visit to the United States comprised a gruelling two-month journey across numerous states, with meetings being held almost every evening, in places including New Jersey, Rhode Island, Kentucky and Minnesota. This represented an extensive workload for Connolly in his attempt to raise funds for the party and, principally, to get subscriptions for the *Workers' Republic*.

While Connolly was in the United States a long-standing member of the ISRP, Murtagh J. Lyng undertook the responsibility of editing the *Workers' Republic*. However, the Kildare man's tenure as editor was cut short by his untimely death on 26 October 1902. According to the obituary printed in the paper, Lyng (who had been born in Athy in 1871, the year of the Paris Commune) died from a rupture of the aorta:

> He had the advantage of an education somewhat above that of the average worker. He was borne to the grave by his comrades and friends, the Red Flag of the revolution draped on his coffin. One of the founders of the party, he was determined to establish a thoroughly class conscious party. Murtagh Lyng was one of its most untiring and unselfish workers.[6]

For such a small organisation the loss of a founding and leading member, who was deeply involved in the production of the *Workers' Republic* in particular, was a major blow. The immediate impact became obvious when the December issue of the paper was not published, due to the combined difficulties of Murtagh Lyng's death and campaigning for the local elections.

Things did not improve for the ISRP when its preparations for the elections, to be held in January 1903, were thrown into chaos after its candidate for the North City Ward, William McLoughlin, had to pull out at short notice because of problems with his electoral registration. Thomas Lyng, the brother of the recently deceased, moved in to fill McLoughlin's shoes. Despite the fact that the party had gathered a lot of experience of electioneering by this stage of its development, the election proved to be disastrous for the party. Lyng received only 102 votes in the North City Ward, compared to the winner who received 736. Connolly, who had returned from the United States, received a fairly derisory 243 votes in the Wood Quay Ward, compared to the winning UIL candidate's total of 763. Connolly's result was an even bigger blow because it showed a fall from the 431 votes he had received in the same ward the previous year. Connolly had had little time to prepare for the election on the ground because he had not returned from the United States until late 1902. Problems regarding the finances of the party were also growing and this did not allow for the best atmosphere in which to conduct an election campaign.

Rather than trying to analyse its electoral setback, the party's official stance, as articulated by Connolly in the pages of the *Workers' Republic*, was to proclaim the results an irrelevance. Connolly simply wrote the elections off as a minor moment in the history of the ISRP:

> Now that the sport of electioneering is over the serious work of the Socialist Propaganda must begin again. These elections are the parade days – the days of mustering and marchings, and shoutings on our side; of lying calumniating, intriguing, bribing and terrorising on the side of our enemies.[7]

If this lack of faith in local elections as a viable instrument of the class struggle had been consistent with the ISRP's position over the years, then Connolly could have been making sense here. However, this political reasoning must have seemed rather unconvincing to the party's members, who had watched the party put its limited means into campaigning during the elections (in part leading to the failure to produce the *Workers' Republic* in December 1902). It could be argued that Connolly did not fully believe what he was writing himself: it was perhaps nothing more than a way of buoying up the shattered morale of his ailing party. His use of humour in describing his own defeat by a candidate, who was an undertaker by profession has a very dark tone to it:

> In Wood Quay the capitalist candidate was a funeral undertaker. His supporters claimed he would honestly strive to put down the death rate. 'If he did', said Connolly, 'he would starve himself to death. When everyday he prays for his daily bread, he prays for somebody to die in order that he may get a job.'[8]

Yet laughing off the election results was not going to breath much confidence into the ranks of the ISRP. Despite Connolly's writings, elections remained an integral part of the ISRP's work and it was not proving very good at them. Indeed, the party still had enshrined in its programme the view that 'the conquest by the Social Democracy of political power in Parliament, and on all public bodies in Ireland, is the readiest and most effective means whereby the revolutionary forces may be organised and disciplined to attain that end'.[9] In earlier electoral campaigns Connolly had been positively evangelical about the importance of the ballot box as the final arbiter in the class struggle. In the excitement following the passing of the Local Government Act 1898 the *Workers' Republic*, under Connolly's editorship, had declared before the municipal elections: 'The social republicans of Ireland step at last from the domain of theory into the realm of practice. The class war enters upon its final political expression. Comrades: To your posts.'[10]

Thus, while Connolly tried desperately to downplay the significance of the ISRP's continued failure at the ballot box, it became increasingly obvious to the party's members, including Connolly himself, that something was wrong with the strategy. Electioneering was fundamental to the ISRP's political project: it came above almost everything else, even the publication of the *Workers' Republic*. The constant failure and fall in its already small vote in municipal elections had a draining effect on the morale of the organisation.

The increasingly poisonous atmosphere in the party was also reflected in the expulsion of two members, which was a new development in the party's history. The party expelled Joseph Treacy on 27 January 1903, for 'assisting the capitalist candidate in the North City Ward election'. John Leon was expelled on 3 February for 'neglecting to vote for the nominee of the ISRP at the North City Ward'.[11] Whether these expulsions were a sign of the new 'sectish' nature of the party is difficult to ascertain. Maybe Connolly had decided to bring a little discipline to his own organisation, the type of discipline that he had witnessed in the SLP while on his speaking tour. The SLP was a party where expulsions were commonplace. It is clear that Connolly's politics were moving further to the left and his conviction of the need for a tightly disciplined party was part of that political shift.

Connolly had returned from the United States to find a party that was far from tightly disciplined. The ISRP's finances were in a dismal state. A licensed bar had been installed in the party's office and the subscription money for the *Workers' Republic* that he had sent home from his speaking tour had been spent on covering the bar's costs. Connolly was overcome with rage and railed against his comrades when he became aware of this situation. Many of his comrades reacted angrily to Connolly's admonishment and he was accused of bullying or 'bossism'.

In February 1903 Connolly proposed the payment of the rent arrears on the party's offices in order to avoid the loss of its press, a Wharfdale printing machine purchased at great expense. Connolly made the case that the party had *Workers' Republic* orders to meet from both American and other subscribers. Connolly lost this argument within the party and tendered his resignation, which was accepted by a majority of the membership:

> We are asked to state that Mr James Connolly, until recently editor
> of the *Workers' Republic* and contributor under the nom-de-plume of
> Spailpin, has resigned from membership of the Irish Socialist
> Republican Party. The reasons given were his disagreements with
> the business administration of the party funds, The resignation was
> accepted.[12]

Thus the *Workers' Republic* baldly declared that the founder and driving
force of the ISRP had left the party. It is worth noting that Connolly
actually contributed a number of articles, including 'Home Thrusts', to
the issue in which this notice appeared, so even in the midst of his
resignation Connolly was still the chief contributor to the paper. A slight
majority of party members, led by Edward Stewart, had turned against
Connolly, his apparent 'bossism' being their unifying grievance.

Weeks later, after Stewart himself had resigned from the party, he
accused Connolly of having effectively held a gun to the members'
heads when he threatened resignation following the majority's
decision not to pay the rent on the party's premises. It seemed to
some party members that, while Connolly may have been right
regarding the financial issues, to tender his resignation just because
his comrades would not agree to what he wanted was an example of
impetuousness to say the least, or even an example of what Stewart
and his followers described as typical bullying on Connolly's part.
However, to understand Connolly's anger one must look at the
changes that had taken place in the financial structure of the *Workers'
Republic* since 1901.

As we have discussed, the paper had continued to be a source of
major problems for the party. It was costly to print and it had had a
rather on-off history. Connolly believed that the paper was central to
the future of the ISRP and in February 1901 it had been decided to
form a Workers' Publishing Company to produce the paper on a
'strictly business basis'.[13] The company was to replace the voluntary
labour that up to then had been the basis of the publication of the
paper. In July 1901 the party decided to sell shares in the Workers
Publishing Company to try to raise funds. The shares had a number
of benefits for the subscribers, the main one being that shareholders
would receive free copies of all the pamphlets produced by the party,
but in the main the scheme was established to help to cover rising
printing costs:

> All shares redeemable by their holders on giving six months notice
> to the management in writing. Subscribers of shares to the value of

£1 in the name of any single individual to entitle that person to free copies of all the literature hereto issued by the Workers' Publishing Company.[14]

The establishment of the company was intended to signal a bright new era for the *Workers' Republic*. Connolly was convinced that the paper could now cover its printing costs from sales and he set about attempting to win as many subscribers as possible. His anger at finding all the money that he had raised for this company being spent on other areas of party activity can be understood only in the context of the major effort he had made in trying to make the paper a success.

It would be wrong to give the impression that all the day-to-day activities of the ISRP ceased during this apparent meltdown. In March 1903 the party held a concert and drama night in the Rotunda in Dublin. Frank Ryan's 'splendid socialist play' *The Laying of the Foundations* was performed. However, one can only guess at the rather caustic atmosphere that must have marked that night, with party members close to being at each other's throats.[15]

Connolly was crushed by what he saw as his unjust treatment at the hands of his comrades, who showed little gratitude for the years of work that he had put into helping to establish the ISRP. He believed that there were other reasons for the strife within the organisation and pointed to underlying causes of the split (which will be discussed later). In a letter to the party, he gave expression to the pain that he was feeling:

> When I recall the fact that this party in Dublin has been built up on sacrifices – sacrifices by many members of their time and energy and spare cash, and by myself of the time and energy and the sacrifice of the commonest necessaries of life to myself and family for nearly five years, then I think I will be exonerated from the charge of egotism in taking this extreme step to arrest the attention of the members before they ruin what has cost so much to build ... In conclusion allow me to say that while I am ready as anyone to laugh at dodging creditors when we have no money, I yet think that the policy of refusing payment when we have the money should not be tolerated.[16]

Connolly was not left out of the party long: after a month of political machinations he rejoined in early March 1903. A general meeting of the party was called for 10 March to discuss his resignation and it was at that meeting the members decided to invite Connolly back into the fold. Stewart, who was in attendance at the meeting, said that it was not an official meeting because he had not been informed in advance in writing that it was to take place. Stewart and his followers who opposed the readmittance of Connolly into the party were then defeated. Stewart resigned and took a number of the younger members of the party, including William O'Brien, with him. The ISRP was irrevocably damaged and even Connolly boasting in the final issue of the *Workers' Republic* regarding the 'counter-revolution' that had occurred in the party could not hide the fact that the ISRP was nearing death's door.[17]

The Secretary presiding over this internal chaos was Tom Lyng. He wrote a letter in the final issue of the *Workers' Republic* outlining the party's 'official view' of the financial issues that had brought the personality conflicts to a final confrontation. Stating that the financial plight of the party would not make pleasant reading, Lyng's account of what had happened to the money raised by Connolly in the United States that provides some context for Connolly's outburst of anger at his comrades. Lyng also made it clear that he did not believe that anything untoward had happened to the money. According to Lyng, the finances had been treated in a careless manner, and incompetence rather than desire for personal enrichment had led to the filtering away of the money:

> As was to be expected in the course of the struggle many debts were contracted the cumulative effect of which bore heavily on the party... The subscriptions sent in – each paying for the paper for the period of one year – were treated as if they were donations.[18]

With Connolly away, working hard to raise subscriptions for the *Workers' Republic*, 500 orders were sent to the party by American and Canadian sympathisers for yearly subscriptions to the *Workers' Republic*. The money that was sent to the ISRP was not competently dealt with. It was treated as if it was up to the party to use as it wished, and thus it was decided, in Connolly's absence, to spend it on covering the ever-rising cost of the bar in the party's offices. The bar was badly run and members did not always pay for the drinks they were having. The bar got a name as a place where cheap or sometimes free drink could be obtained and understandably it became popular among people outside the core party membership. The drink bought for the bar cost money and sales were not covering the cost. The members decided to use the subscriptions sent home by Connolly to cover these costs:

> But here we have the admission to make that those in charge of the
> party finances did not apparently realise their full responsibilities.
> The subscriptions sent in – each paying in advance for the paper for
> the period of one year – were treated as if they were donations; no
> proportion was set aside to enable the party to meet the obligations
> it incurred, except a small sum for postage, and thus each fresh
> subscription became a fresh burden on the party.[19]

Lyng's official account states that by the end of 1902 and the early
part of 1903 the party's financial books became unreliable, as those in
charge of the finances did not deal with them in an appropriate way:

> To such as those in charge of party accounts in the quarter ending
> December 1902 included all subscriptions under income, but
> neglected to set down as liabilities the accompanying obligation to
> produce.[20]

The charges of 'bossism' and inability to work successfully with his
comrades are repeated against Connolly by some of the most
respected historians of the period. J.J. Lee, for example, writes that
Connolly 'was a cankerous man. He had a genius, even in the faction-
ridden company he kept, for quarrelsomeness.' We are also told that
Connolly was too 'abrasive and theoretical'.[21] Edward Stewart and his
followers would have undoubtedly agreed with these views.

In all political organisations there is a constant friction between the
full-time party workers and those who give up their spare time to
work on behalf of the party. Connolly, as a 'full-timer', was demanding
on his comrades, but he called for professionalism while many of his
fellow members were somewhat lax about essential party tasks,
including keeping finances under control. It is interesting to note that
in one of his later theoretical clashes with Daniel De Leon in the United
States Connolly also charged De Leon with excessive 'bossism'. As
Kieran Allen has noted, the term is extremely non-political and
perhaps tends to cover up more fundamental political differences.[22]

Despite this, it seems to be the case that Connolly was not
sufficiently understanding of what he viewed as his comrades' lapses
of judgement and commitment in their dealings as members of the
party. The letters of the ISRP give many examples of the 'dressing
down' that Connolly regularly gave to his comrades. These happened
mainly when Connolly was away from Ireland and the *Workers'
Republic* was not being printed on time (or at all). As early as the
quarterly report issued in the summer of 1899 the party, but

principally Connolly, was questioning the commitment being shown by some of its members:

> ... there has been a most extraordinary lack of activity on the part of the Members of the party, and ... as a result the Party is tottering to ultimate ruin and disaster. The least intelligent must know that as a revolutionary party pledged to take its part in the destruction of the present social organization a great amount is needed to keep it in existence.[23]

Connolly did seem to show a lack of empathy with the everyday problems faced by volunteer members of the organisation. Connolly, who sacrificed so much of his own existence to help the ISRP to carry out its political work could not countenance any perceived lack of commitment on the part of other party members. Considering his background in the rough and tough slums of Edinburgh, coupled with his years serving in the King's Liverpool Regiment of the British Army, Connolly would have had little experience in the gentle coaxing and understanding that is sometimes needed in organisations. Connolly's world was one of sacrifice and commitment: he gave them himself and expected every other member to do likewise.

One of Connolly's biographers, Samuel Levenson, believes that it was the nationality of the people involved that was the fundamental reason for the friction within the ISRP. Connolly the rational Scot found it difficult to work with his Irish comrades because of the supposed Irish love of partaking in intoxicated procrastination:

> Connolly could not tolerate the Irish (perhaps human) fondness for blurring issues, for postponing unpleasant decisions, for engaging in humorous chit-chat and a drink when serious political problems had to be settled.[24]

This rather idiosyncratic reasoning is saved from being truly offensive only by the important caveat that the vices he charges Connolly's Irish comrades with possessing may also be shared by the wider human race, although this seems far from certain. What Levenson's conclusion expresses is the inherent problem in seeking to find personal reasons for the split in the ISRP, rather than trying to uncover the more fundamental sources of the troubles. The above narrative of personality clashes tells us little about the underlying problems that had set the party on this trajectory of destruction. One of the more interesting aspects of the split in the party involves the differing political philosophies that guided the actions of Connolly and his eventual nemesis, Stewart. The pull of Daniel De Leon's radical socialism on the former and the influence of the growing trend towards reformism within the international socialist movement on the latter had a major impact on their parting of the ways.

REVOLUTION VERSUS REFORM

The final months in the history of the ISRP were marred by division, but what are often viewed as simple personality clashes between strong-willed individuals, were in fact little more than reflections of deeper political divisions that were ever widening in the international socialist movement. Connolly said as much at the time. Writing in a letter to his friend Matheson dated 9 March 1903, he observed that the petty in-fighting regarding the financial situation was an echo of much more fundamental divisions:

> The curious thing is that the whole fight is being fought out 'round the corner', so to speak, from the real issue. The only thing that is discussed is that financial situation, and the other point is only noticeable by the fact that all the moderates are aligned against me and all those who have no use for moderation are for me...Of course my position on the finances is sound in itself and I am in dread that as a consequence of their carelessness with the money they will not be able to fill out the American subscriptions...I think that if my side comes uppermost the Kangaroo element will resign, and if they do I may rejoin but it will only be at most a nominal connection in order to keep them together until the angry passions are quiet.[25]

By 'the Kangaroo element' Connolly meant the reformists and moderates gathered around Edward Stewart. The word 'kangaroo' was used at the time as a term of abuse for socialist reformists; it originated from the disputes within the SLP, where the left of the party charged the right with setting up 'kangaroo courts' to expel radical members for the slightest infringement of any rules. The 'moderates' Connolly wrote about were led by Stewart, who had become very involved within the union apparatus in Dublin and was also advocating a closer connection between the party and the contemporary conservative union structures. Interestingly, in his own letter detailing the reasons why he left the ISRP Stewart does not touch on any 'political' issues. Rather Stewart argues that his own resignation from the party followed a personal disagreement over the nature of Connolly's readmittance to the organisation.

> On last February 18th at a meeting of this organisation James Connolly resigned membership because a motion he moved was rejected. That intimidatory action being conduct unworthy of any socialist, and being thoroughly indefensible.[26]

Stewart sent this letter to the SDF's journal *Justice*. Since Connolly had become increasingly hostile to the SDF because of its political shift to the right, this looks like a deliberate attempt by Stewart to anger Connolly. While Stewart was moving closer to the trade unions his own belief in radical socialism was dissipating. He had stopped going to the ISRP's weekly business meetings and, reading between the lines of his resignation letter, it seems as if he wanted any excuse to leave the organisation. Some of his opponents within the party alleged that he had told them that he would 'put the party in the melting pot' and that he would 'wreck it within six months'. It is also instructive to see that members of the party had noticed that Stewart had become 'too busy in the Trades Hall pursuing the reformers policy of "boring from within" wire-pulling to get this or that man an official position'.[27] It seems clear that Stewart's political centre of gravity had moved from playing a central role in the ISRP to partaking in the machinations and political intrigue of bureaucratic trade union life. In contrast, by 1903 Connolly had become increasingly influenced by De Leon's thinking on the role of trade unions and was now more than ever in favour of a 'clear-cut' socialist stance. He thus rejected any moderation in the party's policies and was opposed to working within the bureaucracy of the existing trade unions.

Both Stewart and Connolly were articulating their views a number of years before the arrival of syndicalism and Larkinism in Dublin, which led to tumultuous radical struggles within the Irish working classes. Unions in Dublin during the period of the ISRP's existence were, as we have seen, craft-based and conservative, maintaining a closed shop against unskilled migrating labour. However, with the huge influx of unskilled labourers from the rural areas of Ireland into Dublin after 1904, the more open and radical syndicalist unions led by James Larkin came to the fore.

Both Connolly and Stewart looked at Dublin's union structure as of 1903, and could not, however, foresee the major changes that were to occur in the coming years. Stewart wanted to accommodate with the prevailing circumstances of union life, while Connolly rejected them. Sections of the ISRP supporting Stewart reacted to the party's political isolation by attempting to adapt to the conservative trade-union apparatus and watering down the party's radical agenda. In contrast, Connolly looked to more clear-cut, left-wing politics and a more fundamental rejection of the type of leaders who then led the craft unions.

Many years after the split William O'Brien, who had followed Stewart out of the ISRP, summed up the feelings of those who had wanted the ISRP to have a closer connection to the trade union structure. While recognising the argument of some in the party that the unions were somewhat ineffective in the fight for socialism, O'Brien believed that there was only one strategy open to the party:

> There was a certain justification for this [hostility to craft unions], but all the same the trade union bodies gave an opportunity for pushing socialist principles amongst people who were more likely to respond than the people they would meet at a propaganda meeting.[28]

By March 1903 the ISRP had differing unofficial factions that sought radically different solutions to the party's overall problem of deep political isolation. It would be wrong to see these growing divisions in a purely parochial context, or as being essentially about personality issues or trade union policy. The life span of the ISRP witnessed the early skirmishes between what would eventually be referred to as 'reformist' and 'revolutionary' currents within the international socialist movement.

The late nineteenth century saw the rise of a 'reformist' perspective within the Second International. European capitalism had gone through a period of some prosperity in the final few years of the nineteenth century. There had not been a major slump for a decade and some members of the European socialist movement had begun to believe that capitalism had found a way out from the 'boom and bust' future that Marx and Engels had predicted. During 1897–98 Edward Bernstein, a leading member of the SPD, published a series of articles in the German socialist paper *Die Neue Zeit*. These eventually formed the basis of his book known in English as *Evolutionary Socialism*. He essentially argued that the SPD should be transformed into a party advocating social reforms rather than socialist revolution.[29] The instability within the capitalist system, according to Bernstein, had been tamed by the growth of cartels, trusts and credit institutions that all gradually alleviated the more pernicious effects of the market system on the working class. 'The final goal, no matter what it is, is nothing; the movement is everything', in Bernstein's famous words.[30] Bernstein argued for some sort of clear, blue water between economic and political campaigns, proposing that socialism should be an ideal that the working class should wish for, rather than feel impelled to strive for because of their economic subjection. 'Why represent socialism as the consequence of economic compulsion? Why degrade man's understanding, his feeling for justice, his will?' he asked.[31] The Polish socialist Rosa Luxemburg rejected the reformist policy in her pamphlet *Reform or Revolution* (1899). She defended the overthrow of capitalism and its replacement by socialistic planning as essential components of the socialist project.[32] The debate raged in Germany and eventually engulfed the entire European socialist family:

> The discussion continued within the party and Second International for a number of years. The SPD executive at first encouraged a theoretical discussion and maintained an ambivalent position, but the practical implications of Bernstein's abandonment of a revolutionary perspective could not be ignored for long. The debate spread through-out the entire International.[33]

The arguments in Germany were also reflected in Russia, where Lenin attacked socialists whom he referred to as 'economists'. The economists wished to see social democracy pursue nothing more than trade-union demands (wage increases, better working standards), rather than the overthrow of the capitalist system itself. Lenin described reformism and its rising influence as 'notorious Bernsteinism' and argued in favour of the essential connection between economic and political demands on the part of the working class:

> For the socialist, the economic struggle serves as a basis for the organisation of the workers into a revolutionary party, for the strengthening and development of their class struggle against the whole capitalist system. If the economic struggle is taken as something complete in itself there will be nothing socialist in it.[34]

The ISRP witnessed its own debate on whether the party should travel down the revolutionary or the reformist road towards socialism, but the small size of the party did not allow for such major discussions and debates to take place without fatally destroying the organisation. In the penultimate issue of the *Workers' Republic* (April 1903), Connolly turned his attention to, and his fire upon, the French socialists, who had entered the coalition government in France. The ISRP had stood on the left of the international during the Millerand debate in 1900, and came out firmly against any coalition between socialists and conservatives. Connolly discussed the fact that the leading French Socialist Jean Jaurès, had recently been elected to the position of Vice-President of the French Chamber of Deputies. Rather than seeing this as a major step forward for the international socialist movement, Connolly interpreted Jaurès' accession, as a move on the part of the 'French capitalist class to disorganise the Socialist forces by corrupting their leaders. M. Jaurès is one of the middle class elements, which, by joining the Socialist party in search of a "career", were by virtue of their superior education, enabled to make themselves leaders of the working class movement.'[35] In this concrete example of reformism taking root in the European socialist movement Connolly saw a reflection of a more widespread movement by capitalist politicians to try to disunite the socialists into reformist and more radical revolutionary elements:

> Now that working class movements having grown so formidable as to convince every one that the day of its triumph is within measurable distance, the capitalist government seeks for the weakest part of the Socialist armour that it might destroy the dreaded force and so seeking it finds that this weakest part lies in the vanity and ambition of the middle class leaders. First M. Millerand accepted the bait, now M. Jaurès. In other words the capitalist governments of the world are now adopting and improving upon the policy of corrupting or 'nobbling' the leaders which has enabled the English governing class to disorganise every serious attack upon their privileged position.[36]

Connolly went on to propose that the Irish labour movement could draw lessons from the French model. He compares the tactics employed by the French capitalist class to the Home Rule Party's recruitment of men more associated with the cause of labour 'to confuse the working class who were beginning to distrust the Home Rulers'. These men were little more than 'baits to lure the workers on the official party hook', according to Connolly. The mixed political formation of the Land and Labour League, which had within its ranks both people who were 'professed Socialists and people who antagonised their association from its inception', also worried Connolly. He feared the growing power of reformism in all the major socialist parties in Europe:

> If we except the Socialist Labour Party of the United States, and the Parti Ouvrier of France, there is no Socialist party which does not betray signs of wobbling upon the matter. In Germany the Social Democratic Party has admitted into its ranks in the Reichstag the High Priest of the men who accept such 'gifts from the Greeks', Bernstein; and in many other Continental countries the party is in a state of internal war over the matter. In England no one as yet has been asked into the Cabinet from the Socialist ranks, but there are scores fighting to get in a position to be asked, and hungering to accept.[37]

Considering Connolly's comment that the arguments that had engulfed the ISRP were happening 'around the corner from the real issues', it is easy to see a guarded criticism in this article of the reformist tendency growing within his own organisation. All 'the moderates who were aligned against me' were an echo, in Connolly's ear, of the noisy rise of reformism across the continent. The reformists who gathered around Stewart did not have the literary outlet (or perhaps the ability) to articulate their views on paper, but their actions, Stewart's in particular, showed that they fundamentally questioned the political course that Connolly had mapped out for the party. The continuing isolation and demoralisation of the party meant that Stewart's argument for adaptation to the existing trade union structure, rather than 'clear-cut' socialism, was understandably appealing to a large section of the ISRP's membership. In effect Stewart wanted to see the ISRP turn into a new version of the LEA that had been formed in 1898, a party that would have worked closely with the craft unions and used its influence to raise more moderate demands on behalf of the working class in Ireland.

In early April 1903 Stewart left the ISRP and began his move into more mainstream labour politics. He became deeply involved in the Irish Trades Union Council (ITUC) where he began to wield some powerful influence, serving as Treasurer until 1908. His politics moved sharply rightwards after he left the ISRP, and he later became a major critic of James Larkin and syndicalism. Nevertheless, Stewart's vision for the party in 1903 was extremely enticing for many members jaded by isolation. This, rather than Connolly's alleged 'bossism', was possibly the most significant factor in the acceptance of Connolly's original resignation by the majority of the party's membership. Connolly's vision of the party moving to a more leftist position did not seem appealing to many members of the ISRP, and the reality around them, principally in the form of the party's wretched election results, led many members to question the line that they had taken over the years.

Connolly rejoined the party in March 1903 and Stewart resigned in April. Both of these decisions were democratically accepted by the party, reflecting the fact that the ISRP was almost evenly divided between 'moderates' and 'clear-cuts', with neither side having the stomach for a major theoretical clash. While the 'reform or revolution' debates were never as clearly defined or crystallised within the ISRP as they were within the SPD in Germany, or among the Social Democrats in Russia, the traces of these political trends can be clearly seen within the ISRP. The party was not strong enough in numbers to sustain any substantial debate that could have led to the formation of factions and an eventual split with the creation of two differing but viable political organisations, as with the Social Democrats in Russia in 1903 following the formation of the Mensheviks and Bolsheviks.

The financial problems in the party and the arguments that ensued were thus a manifestation of the much larger and more fundamental theoretical difficulties that were plaguing the international socialist movement at the time. Because of the ISRP's extreme marginalisation, these theoretical discussions were never played out within the party. Both Connolly and Stewart had left the ISRP before it had really begun, and the party drifted into history with few apart from its own members shedding a tear after its ultimate demise early in 1904.

COULD THE PARTY EVER HAVE GROWN?

The final issue of the *Workers' Republic* was published in May 1903. By August of that year Connolly had decided to move himself and his family to the United States, and the ISRP had witnessed two minor purges. First Connolly resigned, then was readmitted; and then the Stewart faction walked out, taking a substantial section of the party with them. The party was shattered, and most of its members were personally and politically crushed after seven years of trying to establish the ISRP as a viable organisation in the Irish political landscape. In September the remaining members effectively voted the ISRP out of existence when they passed a resolution to affiliate the rump of the party to the British SLP and to rename the ISRP the Irish Section of the International Socialist Movement.[38] Despite this affiliation, the remaining members continued to use the name 'ISRP' until the early months of 1904. Later in 1903 Connolly, tired and burned out by his experience with the party, left to become an active socialist in the United States.

Historians have tended to conclude that the ISRP was always a non-starter, because the objective conditions essential for its success did not exist in Ireland during the final decade of the nineteenth century and the early years of the twentieth. Considering that many of those active in labour history have broadly been from the left of the political spectrum, it is understandable that they make much of such objective factors. Certainly, Marxist historians and other writers in the historical materialist tradition believe that, in Engels's words, 'in the final analysis' objective economic factors are the ultimate deter-minants to politics and ideology. In respect of the ISRP, Connolly's biographer Desmond Greaves has made the most succinct statement of this approach. Defending Connolly against those who argue that the ISRP project was a failure, Greaves writes:

> The consistent struggle for socialist and republican principles which Connolly waged on every front open to him is not recognised. His failure to stir a lasting mass movement was due not to his own immaturity but to the immaturity of the objective conditions. He was ahead of his time, not behind it. The I.S.R.P. was limited by the environment in which it grew.[39]

There is a lot of evidence to support this conclusion. Ireland in 1896 was hardly the most advantageous place in which to try to develop a strong and powerful socialist movement. The Irish industrial working class was small in the extreme. Ireland suffered from what the Russian socialist Leon Trotsky later described as 'combined and uneven' development, a direct result of its role as the British Empire's closest and longest-standing colony. The industrial proletariat in Dublin was miniscule, grouped around such firms as Guinness, while the vast majority of labourers in the country were rural. Trotsky used the term 'combined and uneven' development to describe the economic conditions of Russia in 1906, where extremely advanced forms of capitalist development could be found in the urban centres of a country that was predominantly underdeveloped.[40] The investment of international and indigenous capital in a small geographical area allowed industrialisation to take place in the centre of a rural nation. For Trotsky this theory meant that Russia was inherently part of the international capitalist system and therefore the victory of socialism in Russia would not be premature (as the classic Marxist position would have implied up until Trotsky's formulation), provided that it was quickly followed by the introduction of socialism in other, more advanced nations. This insight eventually led Trotsky to propound his theory of 'permanent revolution', which placed socialism firmly in its international context rather than locked inside national boundaries.

Connolly and the ISRP proposed a theory for the justification of socialism in Ireland that came to much the same conclusions as Trotsky's theory of permanent revolution: namely, that even an industrially underdeveloped nation such as Ireland might sustain socialism so long as it became part of an international network of socialist nations. Yet the ISRP reached this conclusion from a theoretical starting point very different from Trotsky. While Trotsky believed that capitalism was developing in Russia, even if it was in an uneven way, Connolly believed that large-scale industrial capitalism could not develop in Ireland. Connolly argued that Ireland would remain primarily an agricultural country, hence his insistence on the need for any future socialist government in Ireland to invest heavily in advanced machinery in order to develop that sector. He described agriculture as the 'one important industry in the country'. A socialist Ireland would trade its agricultural goods for industrial produce from other nations, preferably a socialist Great Britain across the Irish Sea. Thus socialism in Ireland could exist so long as it was complemented by the existence of socialism in other advanced nations.

The city with the highest proportion of wage-labourers in Ireland between 1896 and 1904 was Belfast, which was home to major shipbuilding and linen industries. The fact that the largest city in the north of the island was home to the largest concentration of proletarians served only to highlight another major difficulty for any socialist organisation attempting to grow in Ireland: Belfast was a city split by religious allegiances, with the Orange Order a major obstacle to any attempt to propagate the central ideas of socialism among the Protestant working class. In the south it was Catholicism that held ideological sway among the workers. The ISRP was denounced from the pulpit on a number of occasions and official Catholic theology was deeply opposed to the radical brand of socialism espoused by the party. Indeed, the failure of the short-lived ISRP Belfast Branch to establish itself, because of intimidation of the members of the Orange

Order, and the Cork Branch's permanent problems (with pressure from the local Catholic clergy) serve as handy examples of the difficulties faced by the party in both the north and the south of the island. Yet only a year before the final disintegration of the organisation Connolly was still bullish about the organisation's achievements and future:

> What is the secret of the wonderful progress of this party? The secret lies not in the personality of leaders, nor in the ability of propagandists; it lies in the fact that all the propaganda and teaching of this party was, from the outset, based upon the Class Struggle – upon a recognition of the fact that the struggle between the Haves and the Have Nots was the controlling factor in politics, and that this fight could only be ended by the working class seizing hold of political power and using this power to transfer the ownership of the means of life, viz., land and machinery of production, from the hands of private individuals to the community, from individual to social or public ownership.[41]

Obviously Connolly himself did not believe that the objective conditions were sufficiently negative to prevent the growth of the organisation in Ireland. But then the one thing lacking from Connolly's analysis of the period was a detailed description of exactly why the party had not grown. In Connolly's general propaganda in the *Workers' Republic* the failure of the ISRP to make gains at the polls was principally blamed on the backhanded tactics employed by the party's competitors, rather than any fundamental problem with the ISRP policies or programme.

Nevertheless, while it can be said with certainty that objective factors restricted the growth of the party, such factors alone cannot provide the whole story of the eventual failure of the ISRP. To say that the objective factors made the growth of the party impossible would be to use an extremely reductive form of historical materialism. Indeed, Lenin himself referred to such views as 'objectivist' and an undialectical use of the historical materialist method: 'The objectivist speaks of the necessity of a given historical process; the materialist gives an exact picture of the given socio-economic formation and the antagonistic relations to which it gives rise.'[42] Further, the French Marxist Louis Althusser wrote of the 'relative autonomy of the superstructures' when describing how subjective ideology does not have to be a cast-iron copy of the economic objective conditions within which it develops.[43] The existence of the ISRP, even in its weak state, shows that at least traces of the conditions needed for a socialist party to grow in Ireland must have existed. An intelligent materialist account of the failure of the ISRP must therefore intertwine the subjective as well as the objective factors.

The ISRP came to an end in 1904, yet other socialist organisations in Europe were able to continue to grow, albeit in small numbers. Socialist parties in countries with objective conditions that were far from perfect for helping socialism to prosper – Poland and Russia in particular – were able to survive much longer than the ISRP. While not in any way calling into question the view that economic objective factors 'in the final analysis' provide the broad parameters within which history is made, subjective factors, including the ISRP's tactics and interaction with other political traditions, also proved to be crucial to the party's ultimate failure. As we have seen, the ISRP was not strong enough to withstand the division between the incipient reformist and revolutionary tendencies growing within the organisation, and some subjective decisions and actions taken by the organisation contributed to this lack of strength and rigour within the party.

Some rather minor subjective aspects of internal party life did help to weaken the organisation during its final years. The suspension of educational classes, begun in 1896 and discontinued the following year, was in hindsight a mistake that led to the lowering of the level of socialist consciousness among party members.[44] The classes had brought a high level of political discussion to the party by dealing with topics such as 'Ancient Communism', 'Communist Revolts in the Middle Ages', 'Communist Attempts in the 19th Century', 'The Technical Terms of Scientific Socialism' and 'Celticism and Democracy'. A party with a radical ideology needs a strong and developed level of politics among its party cadre if it is to survive. At one level, socialism is a passionate cry of the oppressed at the inhumanity and inequality of the capitalist system, but it is also a set of ideas that questions the 'common sense' view on everything from human nature to how labour should be organised. Holding this set of ideas, particularly when those who hold them are in a small minority, and the rest of popular and establishment ideology is telling them that they arc wrong, requires a high level of politics to withstand what Connolly would have referred to as 'bourgeois ideology'. In the final years of the ISRP the ideological level of politics among the party's members seemed to have fallen, with Connolly standing head and shoulders above most of his comrades intellectually. This intellectual gap no doubt helped to fuel some petty jealousy among the ISRP's members regarding Connolly's ability. As we have discussed before, Connolly was not always the most tactful of men when dealing with his comrades, but his alleged 'bossism' was more a handy stick for his party enemies to beat him with than anything fundamental to the ISRP's failure to grow. The friction was not just something that appeared in 1903: in March 1900 Connolly had tendered his resignation as Secretary because of the 'growing practice of introducing personal dislikes into the business meetings of the party'. The party did not accept the resignation.[45]

Further, the very fact that the party never broke out of its small base led to a drop in morale as the same old faces turned up at each meeting and carried out the day-to-day work of the ISRP. Particularly after 1900 the party never had the much-needed burst of energy and vigour that every organisation requires, and that results only from the introduction of new faces and new ideas. The active party membership in 1903 was, with very few exceptions, much the same as it had been in 1898, and this led to stagnation and eventual petty infighting. Familiarity bred contempt among many of the comrades.

However, the much more pertinent point of interest for any discussion of the subjective decisions taken by the ISRP, and how these contributed to the failure to grow, is its relationship with the political groupings around it, in particular the advanced nationalists. Connolly's attitude towards republicanism has been a point of major controversy both among historians and within the political left in Ireland ever since his death in 1916. The range of views on the interaction between socialism and republicanism in Connolly's political work in Ireland displays how history can become a battleground for varying political and ideological standpoints.

Some historians have praised the support that the ISRP and Connolly gave to the republican movement. Historians such as Desmond Greaves have argued that the strategy employed by the ISRP, which saw the role of socialists in colonised countries as working as closely as possible with the radical sections of the indigenous nationalist movement towards independence (even if it produced only a capitalist 'independent' Ireland), was the only tactical stance available to the ISRP at the time. For others the ISRP's reluctance to criticise the republicans more forcefully falls in nicely with their own 'stages' view of Irish history, which sees the achievement of socialism in Ireland as possible only after the 'national question' has been completely resolved.[46] Bernard Shaw gave one of the most eloquent statements of the 'stages' position when he argued that an enslaved nation could never turn its mind to anything else until it finds its freedom: 'It will listen to no reformer, to no philosopher and no preacher, until the demand of the nationalist is granted. It will attend to no business, however vital, except the business of unification and liberation.'[47]

As already observed when dealing with the ISRP's attitude to republicans, Connolly's attempt to win over the advanced nationalists to the idea of socialism and his belief that 'true' Irish republicanism was essentially anti-capitalist was built on highly questionable assumptions, first, that capitalism in Ireland was inherently 'foreign' and thus that 'real nationalism' would be 'anti-capitalist', and that second, that full-scale capitalism was impossible in Ireland. Basing its approach to republicans on such unsound theoretical ground was always going to lead to some confusion in the ISRP's dealings with the advanced nationalists.

Whatever one's viewpoint, at least one thing is clear, the ISRP's attempts at winning over republicans to the programme of socialism and the need for a workers' republic, failed utterly. The ISRP did not succeed in winning large or even small numbers of advanced nationalists to the party. While some individual republicans expressed their admiration for the party (Gonne, Milligan) and for Connolly himself (Griffith), they were never won over to the political standpoint of the ISRP. Indeed, if anything, the minuscule numbers of people who moved between the two political movements tended to be ISRP members drifting towards the republicans. After the break-up of the ISRP a small number of the remaining rump found themselves pulled towards Griffith's politics and his growing band of followers. The ISRP under Connolly's direction consistently downplayed the differences between its own politics and that of Griffith and the advanced nationalist movement. While it was both correct and understandable that the ISRP would work alongside republicans in joint mobilisations during such events as the anti-Jubilee protest, or campaign against the Boer War, it was a strategic decision by the ISRP to try to garner support from republicans by not subjecting the advanced nationalists to the type of polemical and stringent criticism that it directed towards other organisations, such as the Home Rule Party or the trade union movement.

The interaction between the ISRP and the advanced nationalists brings into closer focus the whole concept of 'socialist republicanism', which the ISRP was the first organisation in Ireland to espouse. While this study has already investigated what the ISRP broadly meant by socialism, the party's republicanism is a little more difficult to define. Of course the term 'republic' is a historical one that has echoed down the ages, meaning significantly differing things to the ancient Roman Senate, the 'Roundheads' in England in the 1640s and the advanced nationalists in Ireland in the early twentieth century. Indeed republicanism in Ireland meant something very different in 1918 than it had in 1902, after the Proclamation of Easter 1916 and the elections of 1918 had made the 'Republic' a rather more tangible thing. However, at its simplest, republicanism during the period of the ISRP's existence meant separation from the British Empire and an Irish Parliament, elected by the Irish people, replacing the legislative power of Westminster and the symbolic power of the Crown. Beyond that republicanism meant many different things to various political groupings and individuals.

Connolly and the ISRP never provided a class analysis of the republican movement. Connolly believed that republicans could be won over to the cause of socialism because, unknown to themselves, the advanced nationalists held beliefs that could only be realised through the establishment of a socialist Ireland. Connolly massively underestimated the powerful hold that republican politics had over its adherents as well as the complex class nature of republican politics. Connolly seems to have believed that because the republicans were against British imperialism they were all also anti-capitalist, something that was patently untrue. Although many of the adherents to the politics of republicanism were from proletarian backgrounds, republican politics did not of necessity have to be socialistic in nature. The most glaring example of this was Griffith's own economic policies. The ISRP did not recognise how some strands of militant republicanism could actually support Irish capitalism. Despite being arguably one of the finest proponents of the socialist cause the international labour movement has ever known, Connolly was unable to convince a substantial number of advanced nationalists to join the ISRP. The party never viewed the republicans, as it should have done, as competitors for the political allegiance of the Irish working class. The ISRP emphasised what united socialists with republicans in theory, rather than what divided them in practice. It did not view the political conquest of the Irish working class as something that would have brought it into competition with the republicans, and thus it ceded a huge amount of ground to Griffith and his followers. The advanced nationalists never suffered from the same concerns regarding the ISRP and set about the task of building their own power base regardless. Griffith may have given some limited support to Connolly personally, but he was quick to mercilessly criticise the parts of the ISRP's programme, principally the economic and thus the most fundamental policies, with which he did not agree.

History has proved that the ISRP's political orientation towards the republicans, rather than, say, the trade union movement, failed utterly. While the ISRP collapsed the small forces of republicanism grew in strength after 1904 and eventually came to the forefront of the fight for national liberation in subsequent years.

In conclusion it may be said that the difficulty posed by the objective factors in Ireland at the time did indeed prevent the ISRP from growing into a substantial organisation. Ireland then could not have sustained a major socialist party. The support base, which would have had to be comprised of militantly class-conscious industrial workers, was just not in existence in substantial enough numbers on the island. However, to say the party was prevented from growing is a different thing from saying that the ISRP could not have survived. There is little doubt that the party could have survived beyond 1904 if some of the subjective decisions taken by the ISRP and discussed in this chapter had not helped hasten the death of the organisation. As the leading intellectual and activist in the party Connolly must bear much of the responsibility for this, although Edward Stewart and his followers arguably played an extremely negative and destructive role in the organisation in its final years.

Other socialist organisations, notably the Russian Bolsheviks under the leadership of Lenin, were able to survive in sometimes tiny numbers despite splits, constant police intimidation, imprisonment and exile. In the dark days of the Bolshevik Party, years before the October Revolution in 1917, when the organisation numbered a few hundred individuals working undercover in Russia or scattered to the wind across continental Europe, the party was able to overcome huge difficulties to keep the flame burning. In the years following the defeated Russian Revolution of 1905–07 the Bolshevik organisation almost collapsed:

> These were days of very small deeds: a tiny party school abroad was an achievement. To all intents and purposes the party hardly existed ... Lenin kept hundreds of his cadres during the period of reaction, recruited a few more hundred and trained them – always preparing for the future.[48]

The constant attention to organisational detail, the single-mindedness of the Bolsheviks to the socialist cause, and their ability to defend the Marxist tradition and criticise other political trends meant that the party had enough hardened cadres that when the revolutionary days of 1917 came, the organisation had well-respected militants living and working up and down Russia. Because of their influence built up over many years within the working class the party swelled from an organisation of a few thousand to the mass party that led the October Revolution in 1917.

The contrast is made here not simply to argue that if Connolly had been more like Lenin, or the ISRP had been organised on the same basis as the Bolsheviks it too would have been successful. Indeed, it could be argued that Connolly was a superior revolutionary to Lenin in a number of ways and that the organisational lessons that a socialist party working in Ireland during the period could have learned from the almost clandestine work carried out by the Bolsheviks may have been limited. Lenin himself did not believe that the organisational structure of the Bolsheviks had anything to teach the international socialist movement until near the time of the October Revolution. Up until then Lenin, like the rest of the European socialist family including the ISRP, looked to the SPD as the blueprint for organisational structure. Yet it was tightness, centralisation and a strong emphasis on Marxist education that marked the Bolsheviks. Rather than the dictatorial one-man show that some historians have depicted the organisation, the Bolsheviks, in fact, sustained a heaving forum of debate in which Lenin was often in the minority and some of his political stances were held in derision by many of his comrades. However, while there was democracy there was also a centralised leadership that made sure that tasks were fulfilled. This 'democratic centralist' model, in which policy and platforms are debated but when a decision is taken the organisation moves forward as one to implement the decision, was completely lacking in the ISRP. The ISRP in its final years had the worst of both worlds. Many of the party's members did not posses a strong enough understanding of socialism to be able to debate politics with Connolly, so there was little democratic discussion. At the same time the party did not have a centralised structure: rather, the inner workings of the ISRP were marked by an almost complete lack of accountability and massive disorganisation.

The ISRP under Connolly lacked the qualities possessed by the Bolsheviks under Lenin. If the ISRP had survived it would not have led a socialist revolution in Ireland, but it could have grown rapidly in the period of class militancy under the trade union leadership of James Larkin between 1907 and 1913. Instead the party created a space for radical politics in Ireland, particularly in Dublin, that it squandered with its implosion in 1904. The political space created by the ISRP with hundreds of public meetings, copious amounts of printed literature, street protests and electioneering was eventually filled by other groups, particularly Arthur Griffith and his Sinn Féin party.

James Connolly said that his emigration to the United States in 1903 was the 'greatest mistake of my life'.[49] If he had remained in Ireland and carried on his work in the ISRP, even with its tiny numbers, the organisation could have grown and played a significant role in the militant years in Ireland between 1904 and the War of Independence.

NOTES

1. W.K. Anderson, *James Connolly and the Irish Left* (Dublin: Irish Academic Press, 1994), p. 51. This comment would have had a particular relevance for Connolly himself. In May 1904, having been in the United States for just over eight months after leaving Ireland and the ISRP, Connolly waited at Ellis Island for his wife Lillie and his six children to arrive off the boat from Dublin. When he met his family there were only five children: a shattered Lillie had to explain to James that their 13-year-old daughter Mona had died from horrific burns after a kitchen fire on the very day they were due to leave Dublin.

2. James Connolly, letter to John Mulray, quoted in C. Desmond Greaves *Life and Times of James Connolly* (London: Lawrence & Wishart, 1986), p. 148. Connolly had made the same accusation in a letter to Dan O'Brien in June 1903 'Men have been driven out of Ireland by the British Government, and by the landlords, but I am the first to be driven forth by the "Socialists"': quoted in Sean Cronin, *Young Connolly* (Dublin: Repsol, 1983), p. 91.

3. *Workers' Republic (WR)*, Vol. 4, No. 33, March 1902.

4. *WR*, Vol. 4, No. 33, March 1902. At this time Connolly felt the 'little band of pioneers' to be almost an extension of his own self. 'Of course you may say that it was not suggested to me specifically, but to our party, and then only jocularly. But that is just my peculiarity, that I am not able to draw the dividing line between myself and the party.' Letter, James Connolly to Matheson 28 Aug. 1902: William O'Brien MS (NLI) 13,906 (ii). This personal identification with the ISRP made the eventual split in the party all the more difficult for Connolly.

5. *WR*, Vol. 5, No. 3, Sept. 1902. The idea of an American speaking tour by an ISRP member had been around for a number of years. 'The first

request for an Irish agitator to tour America came from Henry Kuhn, National Secretary of the SLP, shortly after the formation of the organisation (ISRP) in 1896.' Letter, James Connolly to Owen Cullen, Secretary of the Socialist Party of Ireland (SPI), 29 April 1907: William O'Brien MS (NLI) 33,718/B (29).

6. *WR*, Vol. 5, No. 5, Nov. 1902.
7. *WR*, Vol. 5, No. 7, February 1903.
8. Ibid.
9. ISRP 1896 Programme, Appendix One.
10. *WR*, Vol. 1, No. 11, 22 Oct. 1898.
11. *WR*, Vol. 5, No. 7, Feb. 1903.
12. *WR*, Vol. 5, No. 8, March 1903. While Connolly did not say so in the debates surrounding the party's financial problems, the fact that a bar, in particular, was established inside the headquarters of the ISRP must have really irked him. A lifelong teetotaller, he believed that the 'demon drink' was the ruin of many a working-class life and once rather optimistically boasted that a 'drunken Socialist is as rare as a white blackbird': *Socialism Made Easy* (Dublin: The Plough Book Service, 1971), p. 30.
13. *WR*, Vol. 4, No. 23, Feb. 1901.
14. *WR*, Vol. 4, No. 28, July 1901.
15. *WR*, Vol. 5, No. 8, March 1903.
16. Connolly, letter to the ISRP, quoted in Cronin, *Young Connolly* (Dublin: Repsol, 1983), pp. 82–3.
17. *WR*, Vol. 5, No. 9, April 1903. The bitterness that Connolly felt towards Edward Stewart and the moderates ('kangaroos') becomes clear only in his private correspondence: 'This is the outcome of our little Kang episode. We squelched the reptiles, but they dissimilated so well that, as you saw, my kindly intention to drag their scalps around as a trophy in the public gaze was frustrated and I have no doubt they will be allowed to crawl back': Connolly in a letter to Matheson, 8 April 1903, quoted in Cronin, *Young Connolly*, pp. 87–8.
18. *WR*, Vol. 5, No. 9, April 1903.
19. Ibid.
20. Ibid.
21. Joseph Lee, *The Modernisation of Irish Society (1848–1918)* (Dublin: Gill & Macmillian, 1973), p. 150.
22. Kieran Allen, *The Politics of James Connolly* (London: Pluto Press, 1990), p. 76.
23. Minutes, 10 July 1899, in Minutes of the Irish Socialist Republican Party, 1898–1904, MS 16264–67, O'Brien Collection, National Library of Ireland (NLI).
24. Samuel Levenson, *James Connolly, Socialist, Patriot and Martyr* (London: Quartet, 1977), p. 103.
25. James Connolly, letter to Matheson, 9 March 1903, quoted in Cronin, *Young Connolly*, p. 86.
26. *WR*, Vol. 5, No. 9, April 1903.
27. Ibid.
28. William O'Brien, *Forth the Banners Go* (Dublin: Three Candles, 1969), p. 36.

29. See Edward Bernstein, *Evolutionary Socialism* (Stuttgart: SPD, 1899).
30. Mary-Alice Waters (ed.), *Rosa Luxemburg Speaks* (New York: Pathfinder Press, 1970), p. 36.
31. Tony Cliff, *Rosa Luxemburg* (London: Bookmarks, 1986), p. 27.
32. Ibid. pp. 25–34.
33. Waters (ed.), *Rosa Luxemburg Speaks*, p. 35.
34. Quoted in Tony Cliff, *Lenin: Building the Party (1893–1914)* (London: Bookmarks, 1994), pp. 63–64.
35. *WR*, Vol. 5, No. 9, April 1903.
36. Ibid.
37. Ibid.
38. Minutes, 4 Sept. 1903.
39. Greaves, *Life and Times*, p. 167. Probably the first writer to try to look at the failure of the ISRP both objectively and subjectively was D.R. O'Connor Lysaght: 'The ISRP had to work under conditions both objective and subjective that made a Socialist revolution in Ireland more of a hazard than it was in any other nation in the North Atlantic seaboard. Class relationships there were underdeveloped in connection with both external relationships and internal confrontations... The lack of economic development meant a lack of industry... Thus the Irish proletariat was bound to be less disciplined to mass action and less politically developed': D.R. O'Connor Lysaght, in Connolly, 'Introduction', *Socialism Made Easy* (Dublin: The Plough Book Service, 1971), p. 5.
40. See the chapter 'Peculiarities of Russia's Development' in Leon Trotsky, *The History of the Russian Revolution* (London: Pluto Press, 1977).
41. *WR*, Vol. 4, No. 33, March 1902.
42. Lenin, quoted in John Rees, *The Algebra of Revolution: The Dialectic and the Classical Marxist Tradition* (London: Routledge, 1998), p. 172.
43. See Louis Althusser, *For Marx* (London: Norton, 1996).
44. Priscilla Metscher, *James Connolly and the Reconquest of Ireland* (Minnesota: Marxist Educational Press/Nature, Society and Thought, 2002), p. 30.
45. Minutes, 5 March 1900.
46. Greaves, *Life and Times* is the best example of this 'stages' view in relation to a study of Connolly's life.
47. Bernard Shaw quoted in Peter Berresford Ellis, *A History of the Irish Working Class* (London: Pluto Press, 1996), p. 10. Berresford Ellis's own views are also classical 'stages' essentially arguing that socialism was not on the agenda until the national question was resolved: 'In Ireland today, as in previous centuries, the mainspring of Socialism is in the national struggle': Ellis, *A History*, p. 7.
48. Cliff, *Lenin: Building the Party*, pp. 292–3.
49. Connolly to O'Brien, 24 May 1909, MS 13908 (NLI), quoted in Allen, *The Politics of James Connolly*, p. 95.

CHAPTER SIX

The Legacy

LIFE AFTER THE ISRP

In one sense the ISRP died in the summer of 1903, with the departure of the faction led by Edward Stewart, coupled with Connolly's eventual departure to the United States in September. Yet a small rump remained and continued to meet under the name of the ISRP until February 1904.

Because of the bad feeling and bitter taste left after the split in the ISRP, Connolly left the city he had worked so strenuously in for the previous seven years to build a secure future for socialism, with not one Dublin socialist there to wave goodbye. Before his departure a special meeting of the ISRP, held in July 1903, had tried to reunify the remaining faction and Stewart's followers, but this attempt failed, despite the pleadings of a number of party members. Thomas Lyng implored the party to reunify despite all differences and work together like the much larger SPD in the case of Germany 'where the movement contains men who were opposed to one another personally, but could work together in fighting the common enemy and helping to build up the movement'.[1] The party carried on holding business meetings, but, as can be garnered from the rather sparse minutes, the level of activity had greatly lessened and membership of the party had crumbled.

After the summer of 1903 the organisation was little more than a name with only a few contacts with other organisations and little or no money. It seems that one of the main factors fuelling the spirit of the remaining members of the party was a shared desire not to give those who had walked out with Stewart the satisfaction of 'winning'. A narrow sectarianism born out of political defeat and the legacy of bitter in-fighting led to the remaining rump becoming a completely isolated entity. It seems that their hatred of Stewart and the 'splitters' was almost their only unifying cause. However, they also felt a strong loyalty to Connolly, who, they believed, had been badly treated by Stewart and his faction. At a party meeting in August 1903 the members of the ISRP passed the following resolution:

> The best appreciation of Connolly's work for Socialism in this country we can offer him is to carry on the work of socialist propaganda by the party which he founded and for which he sacrificed so much; be it further resolved that we consider the actions of those men who have set about forming another party treacherous to the interest of Revolutionary Socialism and an insult to the man and the principles he believes in.[2]

Amid the collapse of the ISRP the remaining members of the party did try to re-start the public meetings at Foster Place, but these meetings began to attract a much more intimidating crowd. Sadly, scuffles between members of the ISRP and those who had left the party with Stewart sometimes occurred:

> An attempt was made to hold a public meeting in Foster Place, College Green. When the men arrived they found an opponent holding a meeting of his own. A meeting was started in opposition, but the platform was rushed and broken to pieces [and] several of the members had to fight for their lives.[3]

To add to the confusion, Stewart and his small group of followers had begun to call themselves the Socialist Labour Party, but it was an organisation in name only. The party held no regular meetings, produced no written propaganda and had no visible street presence.

Further exploratory talks in the early months of 1904 regarding a proposed merging of the two groups faltered because those who had stayed insisted on the retention of the title ISRP. One such meeting took place in February 1904 with the ISRP represented by Patrick Dunne, John Brannigan and William McLoughlin while the SLP was represented by Thomas Brady and William O'Brien. The poverty of ideology and politics within the two rumps can be seen by the fact that these discussions towards 'unity' were not much concerned with major points of socialist politics: rather, the name of the organisation became the fundamental point of disagreement. William O'Brien and the others who were now outside the organisation refused to countenance the use of the title ISRP, thus exposing the deep bitterness that still existed months after the split of 1903. Edward

Stewart had by this stage all but deserted his followers and was concentrating on building his career in the craft unions.

Finally it was decided that the two groups would merge under the new banner of the 'Socialist Party of Ireland' (SPI). The inaugural meeting of this new party took place on 15 March 1904.[4] The SPI was to play a very marginal role during the upsurge in labour unrest in James Larkin's years as a union leader. Like the ISRP, it was to suffer from lack of members as well as financial problems, and its theoretical significance in the history of the Irish labour movement is far less than that represented by the ISRP. Indeed, the SPI actually adopted the programme of the ISRP, with the exclusion of the clause calling for the nationalisation of railways and canals.[5] The SPI believed that this point of the ISRP programme represented a 'centrist demand' that would confuse the workers and take their eyes off the ultimate goal of socialism. As this clearly suggests, the early years of the SPI were marked by a strong ultra-leftist stance in theory, combined with a lack of activity in practice.

Most of the same faces that had been in the leadership of the ISRP also took up leading roles in the SPI. In particular, Dan O'Brien and his younger brother William O'Brien came to the forefront of the organisation. Some of the other leading members of the ISRP were, however, expelled from the SPI. Edward Stewart and William McLoughlin, for example, were expelled for supporting the Home Rule MP and Lord Mayor of Dublin, J.P. Nannetti, at election time.[6]

The SPI had been formed at the beginning of a period when socialists in Ireland were turning their attention to building trade unions as a weapon to defeat capitalism, rather than building a party. This was the beginning of the increasing role for syndicalism in labour politics. The Irish left was now focusing on the 'economic' struggle rather than the 'political' struggle. This was a complete reversal of the ISRP's priorities of just a few years before.

In 1903 and 1904 many former members of the ISRP drifted away from politics altogether, although some of them went on to leave their mark on subsequent Irish political history. What eventually happened to James Connolly in particular became literally the stuff of legend and has been chronicled in forensic detail in numerous accounts of Ireland's foremost socialist writer and agitator.[7] Having spent a sometimes fruitful but eventually disheartening seven years in the United States, Connolly returned to Dublin in 1910, to a very different labour scene than that which he had left behind in 1903. While the ISRP had had to deal with an extremely conservative union structure, Dublin by 1910 was witnessing the growing influence of James Larkin and the syndicalist desire to create 'one big union' that would encompass all sections of the Irish working class, and fight for political as well as economic demands, Connolly became heavily involved in Ireland's first major set-piece class battle during the 1913 lock-out, but its eventual defeat was a blow to the growing confidence of organised labour in Ireland.

Faced with the obscenity of capitalist war on the battlefields of Europe during the First World War, Connolly was shaken by the failure of the major parties of the Second International to stand up against this imperialist conflict. With little organisation around him, apart from his small workers' militia, the Irish Citizen Army (ICA), he became increasingly convinced of the need for a military blow to be struck against British imperialism in Ireland while British troops were engaged in war on the continent. Unlike in the period of the Boer War, there was at least a section of the 'advanced nationalist' movement that was now sufficiently armed and in favour of taking such action. Working closely with Padraig Pearse, Connolly and the ICA joined forces with a minority of the nationalist movement in the Easter Rising of 1916. While this has been viewed by many historians as a foolhardy venture, inspired by thoughts of 'blood sacrifice' for Connolly, the Rising was, at least in its early planning, a logical reaction to the presence in Ireland of a capitalist empire that had politically and ethically lost its right to exist for many years, and had confirmed its inherent inhumanity on the fields of the Somme and elsewhere.

The Rising failed and Connolly, unable to stand because of injuries received while defending the General Post Office on O'Connell Street, was strapped to a chair and executed by the British authorities. Alongside Connolly many of the other nationalist leaders of the rising were also executed, leading left-wingers then and since to question how a strong socialist such as Connolly could have died in what seems like nothing more than a nationalist uprising. Yet some in the international socialist movement did understand the reasons for the Rising. Lenin, for one, praised the bravery of the rebels of 1916, only adding, sadly, that the Rising had taken place too early for the rest of the European revolution, and was thus left isolated. He rejected the view of those socialists who had written of the Rising as nothing more than a 'putsch' and argued that socialists must support any sort of rebellion that dealt a blow to imperialism, even one not led by socialists:

To imagine that social revolution is conceivable without revolts of small nations in the colonies and in Europe, without revolutionary outbursts by a section of the petty bourgeoisie with all its prejudices, without a movement of the politically non-conscious proletarian and semi-proletarian masses against oppression by landowners, the church, and the monarchy, against national oppression, etc. – to imagine all this is to repudiate social revolution.[8]

Nevertheless, there can be little doubt that Connolly had lowered the red flag somewhat during 1916. He went into the Rising in a weak position, having no political organisation around him, apart from the small number of volunteers in his workers' militia. The reasons for the absence of a strong political party that shared his political views can be traced back to the period principally covered by this study. The failure of the ISRP to grow in Ireland set in train the series of events that led to the forecourt of Kilmainham Prison where one of the most extraordinary men in modern Irish history met his fate.

Compared to Connolly the other members of the ISRP have tended to fade into the historical distance. While none has garnered the same amount of attention as Connolly, it is possible nonetheless to trace the historical footsteps of some of them.

Edward Stewart, Connolly's great rival in the final months of the party, followed a political trajectory that was almost the complete opposite of Connolly's. Stewart, as has already been noted, had moved very close to the Irish trade union bureaucracy in 1903. In that year he began to concentrate on the trade unions and even before the split with Connolly he had started to miss the ISRP's business meetings. Later in the decade Stewart served as Treasurer and Secretary of the ITUC, and he became a major opponent of Larkin during the period of Larkin's union activity in Dublin.[9] Stewart then joined the UIL, the organisation once so derided by the ISRP, and won a seat for the UIL on Dublin City Council, where he continued his feud with Larkin. Stewart even wrote a polemical attack on Larkin, entitled *History of Larkinism*, after the 1913 lockout. Stewart's actions in 1903 had given an early indication of how he would live out the rest of his life. Moving rapidly to the political right, Connolly's nemesis ended up as an enemy of the type of radical socialism that he had once espoused and stood as an election candidate for.

William O'Brien, who was one of the youngest members of the

party became a major player in the mainstream trade union movement in Ireland after 1903. He was part of the union leadership throughout the Larkin period and after Connolly's death was one of the leading members of the Irish Labour Party alongside Thomas Johnson. He went on to become one of the most recognisable faces of Irish Labour in the early decades of the Irish Free State. While he remained proud of his role working alongside Connolly, it is questionably how much O'Brien contributed after his mentor's death to Connolly's vision of the establishment of a workers' republic in Ireland. O'Brien was a central figure in what was, by European standards, a very conservative labour movement in the 26 counties.

Con O'Lyhane, the irrepressible ISRP man in Cork, went on to have a rather varied history in the labour movement. Having left the ISRP in 1902, he travelled to Great Britain where he became one of the founding members of the Socialist Party of Great Britain in 1904. He became the party's General Secretary, but was expelled during internecine fighting and subsequently travelled to the United States. There he was welcomed with open arms by the labour movement and worked with Larkin during his stay in the United States after 1913. O'Lyhane was arrested for his opposition to the Great War and died in a New York hospital on New Year's Eve 1919, just after being released from prison.[10]

Most of the other members of the ISRP, like the vast majority of us, became historical nonentities. Some who remained in politics moved into the milieu of advanced nationalism after 1903, while others continued to carry the flame of socialism with the formation of the SPI in 1904.

A 'second' ISRP was founded in Belfast in the 1950s and it won a seat in the Stormont Parliament after its leader, Harry Diamond, topped the poll in the Fall Division.[11] While this party looked to Connolly's ISRP as its forerunner, there was no direct connection between the two organisations. Like an echo in history, the Belfast ISRP petered out as another dead end in the political development of the Irish labour movement.

While the ISRP had come to an end in February 1904, as with most political organisations it helped to spawn a further political entity, in this case the SPI. However, despite its weaknesses, the ISRP spawned not only another organisation but a whole political tradition.

THE SHADOW OF THE ISRP ON THE LABOUR MOVEMENT

The use of 'family trees' in historical studies is something that must be approached with the utmost care. While an organisation may lay claim to a particular political lineage, these public claims may mask an open break between the actual politics of the organisation and its predecessors. In the case of the modern socialist movement in Ireland, this is very much the situation.

The immediate genealogy of the ISRP's descendants is as follows. The SPI remained in existence, with a very low level of activity, until Connolly's return to Ireland in 1910. Connolly joined the SPI, but by that stage, following his experience as a member of the SLP in the United States, he had come to believe that another, less radical organisation should also be formed. This organisation would be based more around the trade union movement and would include socialists of all types. He got his wish in 1912 when the ITUC formed the Irish Labour Party, a forerunner of the modern Labour Party. A number of former members of the ISRP were closely involved in the formation of the Labour Party, including Connolly and William O'Brien, and many other members of the SPI who were also former members of the ISRP held dual membership. The Labour Party was even less active than the SPI, however, and remained more or less dormant until after Connolly's death. In 1921, under the influence of the Russian Revolution of 1917, the SPI was renamed the Communist Party of Ireland, with Connolly's son Roddy Connolly as one of its leading members. Thus the ISRP gave birth to both the reformist socialist movement in Ireland represented by the Irish Labour Party and the more revolutionary strand represented by the various communist parties that have existed throughout the history of the state.[12]

The genealogy of the republican and nationalist movement in Ireland followed a rather different route. All the republican and nationalist parties formed after the creation of the Irish Free State could trace their lineage back to Griffith's Sinn Féin party, formed in 1905. However, many who have stood in that tradition have agreed more with the radical socialistic programme of the ISRP than with the capitalistic economic plans espoused by Griffith. The tradition of 'left republicanism' was created by the ISRP and continues to have some bearing on the wider republican and nationalist movement in Ireland.

The ISRP has thus had a profound influence on that strain of Irish radical politics where some notion of socialism has combined with the most left-wing elements of the republican movement. Sometimes incoherent and often quarrelsome, this strand of socialist republicanism has given the Irish political scene some of its most gifted people, and some of its most interesting, progressive and, sometimes, destructive political formations. The IRA in the 1930s, Saor Éire, the Republican Congress, Clann na Poblachta, People's Democracy, Sinn Féin in the 1980s, and many individuals, such as Peader O'Donnell or Noel Browne, have all been in some way formed, or at least influenced by the tradition of politics created by the ISRP. This radical strand of politics may have represented much that was progressive and admirable, but it also passed on the confusion and problems that contributed to the demise of the party in 1904. This confusion has continued to haunt 'left republicanism' in Ireland ever since.

The problems of this set of politics are very much a legacy of Connolly's and the ISRP's attempts to engage with the republican movement. Irish republicanism may be against British imperialism, but it is not inherently anti-capitalist. This is something that the ISRP, and Connolly, in particular, failed to understand. Irish republicanism has based its political strategy on two central tactics. First, it has the idolisation and use of the gun, something that Connolly criticised in the pages of the *Workers' Republic* as long ago as 1899. Second, republicans have tried to build all-class alliances by seeking to win allies in the nationalist wing of the establishment in Ireland and, in recent years, the political establishment in the United States. Again, this was something that Connolly criticised during his period in the ISRP. Neither tactic has anything to with what that is fundamental to socialist politics: the mass mobilisation of the working class. Irish workers are treated as passive onlookers while a special group of guerrillas carry on the 'armed struggle' and/or republican politicians build support among sections of the political elite. With the creation of an all-class alliance or pan-nationalist front Irish republicans have lined up alongside political groupings and individuals that would be seen as 'class enemies' by most socialists. As Kieran Allen has written, when summing up Connolly's relationship with the tradition of republicanism:

> The problem lies in the very nature of republicanism. It is not a working-class ideology, despite the fact that many of its adherents are drawn from the working class. As a set of politics it does not promote the organised power of the working class. Indeed, it is extremely cynical on the potential for workers' organisations in Ireland. Its more left-wing adherents may support strike action, and

even play an active role in some strikes, but this sits uncomfortably alongside an overall republican outlook which denies that the working class are a political force, capable of destroying partition by entering into a fight with both native and foreign capital in Ireland.[13]

While Connolly and the ISRP were right to fight alongside republicans on some issues, they should not have diluted their own politics in an attempt to win the adherence of republicans. They should have struck together but marched separately, keeping their own politics and organisation separate. The legacy of their tactics towards republicanism has meant that many socialists have seen their role as nothing more than political advisers or cheerleaders to the republican movement.

The lack of a strong independent socialist party that fought for workers' control of the economy and the end of British rule in Ireland is also a legacy of the ISRP's tactics. The 'socialist republican' tradition has tended to try to win more mainstream republicans over to a left-wing position by emphasising what they agree on, but in the main this has failed. Like Connolly and the ISRP, modern 'left republicanism' has not won mainstream republicans over to the vision of a workers' republic in an Ireland free of capitalism. They have failed because, just like the ISRP, they misjudge the modern republican movement, as an anti-capitalist movement rather than the anti-British imperialist movement that it is. Socialist republicans have also, just like the ISRP, utterly failed to recognise the powerful hold of tradition that mainstream republican politics has over its adherents. Modern Irish republicans have gone through armed struggle, imprisonment, hunger strikes and internment, and few will leave that tradition to join the small forces fighting for a workers' republic just because of an ideological conversion.

The best strategy for those who have continued to fight for a workers' republic, a strategy that the ISRP could have employed, would be to concentrate on building their own political forces. While working with republicans on issues that they agree about, the ISRP could have criticised the advanced nationalists on those parts of their programme that they did not accept. In doing so they could have forged a socialist tradition in Ireland that would have rivalled the republican tradition. While sticking to an anti-imperialist agenda, the ISRP's vision of a secular workers' republic might even have won the adherence of sections of the Protestant working class, something that the mainstream republican tradition could never achieve.

In response to the outbreak of the Troubles in Northern Ireland in the late 1960s there has been another reaction on the left in Ireland to the republican movement that has been, arguably, more destructive to the socialist cause than the 'left republicanism' strategy employed by others. This more recent response (at least in this author's view) can claim absolutely no legacy from Connolly or the politics of the ISRP. Some on the Irish left have criticised republicans as 'reactionary' and sometimes even 'fascist' because of their use of the armed struggle. Essentially, the more mainstream left in Ireland has abandoned anti-imperialism as a central component of their beliefs. Such a strategy marks a complete break from the radical political tradition launched by the ISRP in 1896.

However, the lesson that should be learned from the failure of the ISRP is that socialism in Ireland must concentrate on building up its own forces, rather than attempting to 'piggy back' on, or gently trying to convince, other traditions. Socialism in Ireland should see the 'mainspring' of its potential success as coming, not from the republican tradition, but rather from the class struggle that continues between workers and the establishment on both sides of the border. Only by the building of a strong, credible and independent socialist party will republicans be convinced to join the struggle, not just for an 'independent Ireland' but for a socialist workers' republic.

CONCLUSION

Physically and emotionally exhausted by the traumas of the Kitty O'Shea divorce trial the previous year, Charles Stewart Parnell travelled around Ireland in 1891 making speeches and meeting Irish people who were no longer his unquestioning supporters. He was attacked physically and verbally, but the reaction he received in Dublin was much more favourable than in the rest of the island, and this gave Parnell hope: 'I rely on Dublin. Dublin is true. What Dublin says to-day Ireland will say to-morrow.'[14]

For much of its existence the ISRP must have hoped for the same sort of foresight on the part of the population of Ireland's capital, because the party remained an almost exclusively Dublin-based phenomenon. While it was very small compared to other political groups, the ISRP was very much part of the political scene in Dublin between 1896 and 1904. The party had an extremely visible presence in both street politics and in local electioneering.

However, its failure to spread its organisation to other cities was a fatal problem that the party was never able to overcome. If the party could have dealt successfully with the clerical difficulties in Cork, it had in Con O'Lyhane a member who could have made a huge impact on politics in the 'rebel city'. In Belfast the ISRP simply did not expend enough energy on building a base within either the Catholic or the Protestant working class. Compared to the huge amount of time, effort and bravery shown by the ILP and the SDF in the early 1890s (and they failed to create strong organisations in that city), the ISRP really did not sacrifice enough in attempting to build socialism in Belfast. This failure was not just one that weakened the party in the short term; in the longer term it contributed to the absence of a strong socialist alternative based on class politics in Belfast, which remained a city where community and religious allegiances were extremely strong within the working class. Thus 'what Dublin says', through the limited support the ISRP received in the capital, was not a sign of further growth for the party across the county.

Despite this geographical limitation, in terms of the written word the party was relatively successful. Considering the size of the organisation, the *Workers' Republic* was a quite impressive production. Its place in the history of radical Irish journalism has never been fully appreciated, but the wide sweep of its international coverage, combined with its more local news items, mark it out as a significant publication in the annals of the Irish labour movement. Connolly can take most of the credit for this, and it was in the pages of the *Workers' Republic* that he first published some of his most famous literary offerings, including his classic *Labour in Irish History*.

The ISRP's relationship with the trade union movement in Dublin was one of the chief factors contributing to its failure to grow. Of course, some of the mistakes made by the ISRP could not have been avoided, but nevertheless the failure to engage with the trade unions in the early years of the organisation meant that the ISRP was never able to build a significant support base within the industrial working class in Dublin. If the ISRP had given more practical support to the striking tailors and dockers in Dublin in 1899 and 1900 it might have won the respect of key militants within these unions, but because it stood by the orthodoxy of the Second International, which argued that strikes were mere distractions for a working class that should be concentrating on socialism, the party never built a base among the workers. Ironically, when sections of the party eventually decided to become more involved in trade union politics in 1902–03, they did so in a most conservative way, looking to the bureaucracy as the most beneficial space from which to push forward the cause of social justice.

The ISRP was extremely unfortunate in having been formed in the a period of conservative craft unionism. If it had survived to see the major rise in union militancy under the leadership of James Larkin, the ISRP might have influenced and won support among the organised working class in the growing ITGWU.

The lack of interest in building support among the unions was matched only by the ISRP's enthusiasm for fighting elections. Yet, while the unions could have provided a good soil from which the party might have grown, the election stage was tilted very much in favour of the more conservative sections of society, which had the financial backing of the capitalist class. The party invested so much money and so many man-hours in fighting elections that the continued failure to win a seat at municipal level was a crushing blow for members to take. The party had a 'Plan A' and it was not working: the split in 1903 was very much about what 'Plan B' should look like.

The notion of winning support among Irish republicans was probably more central to the ISRP's strategy than anything else. As we have already noted, this too failed, with the republicans going from strength to strength after 1904 and the ISRP becoming a historical footnote. The concept of 'left republicanism' that was handed down to the Irish radical tradition by the ISRP has fostered some of the greatest fighters for progressive politics in Ireland, but it has also led to confusion and defeat. The ISRP lacked a class analysis of Irish republicanism: rather than seeing it as a rival for the hearts and minds of the Irish proletariat, the party believed that the advanced nationalists were fundamentally socialistic, even if they were unaware of this. In hindsight this flawed use of a type of 'false consciousness' argument has proved to be counter-productive for the socialist movement in Ireland. While recognising which issues socialists should fight alongside republicans, the ISRP never subjected the republicans to any sustained criticism. Yet the attempt to win republicans over to socialism went on to greatly influence socialists working in Ireland in later decades.

For many the politics of the ISRP will seem to have nothing to tell us about contemporary Ireland. Those who write off socialism as uniquely old-fashioned, and unable to deal with the economic and social problems of the twenty-first century, should ask themselves, however, whether the ISRP's political programme has more relevance now than the policies of their contemporaries? The struggle for limited self-rule for Ireland while staying within the confines of the British Empire, the goal of the Home Rule Party, would undoubtedly garner little support in contemporary Ireland. The UIL's desire to keep as many people as possible on the land, with smallholdings providing the bedrock of economic prosperity, is also rather untenable in today's Ireland. Even the economic protectionist model proposed by the original Sinn Féin under Arthur Griffith would not be easy to implement in a world economy made up of global markets and the free movement of capital. Yet the ISRP's programme, based around the minimum demands of economic redistribution, a shorter working week, public control and management of national schools, and the separation of Church and state, still stands as a set of measures that could be implemented. The system that the ISRP was fighting against, capitalism, remains in place and the more destructive qualities of that system, war and imperialism, are sadly still with us. The party's maximum programme for a workers' republic in Ireland and international socialism abroad are not on the agenda in the short term, but can the righteousness of the cause be questioned when capitalism continues to fail to feed a huge portion of the world's population, condemns millions to grinding poverty and hellish working conditions, sees more and more people even in the Western democracies becoming increasingly disillusioned and detached from the political process, and produces the great death economy represented by the international arms trade?

Despite its failures the ISRP remains a pivotal organisation in the history of the Irish labour and socialist republican movement. Its stance against imperialism, its ability to view the 'national' question in a socialist context and its constant struggle for a workers' republic in Ireland, a republic that would rid the island of all forms of oppression and inequality, and herald a new era for radical democracy, remains an important source of inspiration for those who continue to struggle for socialism in Ireland today. James Connolly and his comrades attempted, but eventually failed, to build a viable party in Ireland that could fight for social justice and socialism. A century on from the demise of the ISRP, the building of that sort of party remains the principal task for socialists in Ireland today.

NOTES

1. Minutes, 6 July 1903, in Minutes of the Irish Socialist Republican Party, 1898–1904, MS 16264–67, O'Brien Collection, National Library of Ireland (NLI).
2. Minutes, 27 Aug. 1903.
3. Minutes, 26 April 1903.
4. Priscilla Metscher, *James Connolly and the Reconquest of Ireland* (Minnesota: Marxist Educational Press/Nature, Society and Thought, 2002), p. 93. Just prior to the unity meeting the Secretary of the SLP, Thomas Brady, wrote to James Connolly in the United States informing him that the two groups were to merge. 'As the founder of the ISRP you will perhaps regret its disappearance. But it is apparent that some sacrifice is necessary to obtain and ensure unity': Letter from Thomas Brady to James Connolly (no date), February 1904 William O'Brien MS (NLI) 15,674 Folder (6).
5. Ibid., p. 95. The Irish SLP did produce a one-page outline of its 'political objectives' however, this was a very general document and had little impact on the framing of the SPI's political programme: *Socialist Labour Party Declaration of Principals* (Dublin, SLP, 1904). (NLI) LO P109 (27).
6. Sean Cronin, *Young Connolly* (Dublin: Repsol, 1983), p. 93.
7. Notably, Kieran Allen, *The Politics of James Connolly* (London: Pluto Press, 1990), W.K. Anderson, *James Connolly and the Irish Left* (Dublin: Irish Academic Press, 1994), C. Desmond Greaves, *The Life and Times of Connolly* (London: Lawrence & Wishart, 1971), Samuel Levenson, *James Connolly, Socialist, Patriot and Martyr* (London: Quartet, 1977), Austen Morgan, *Political Biography of James Connolly* (Manchester: Manchester University Press, 1988), Metscher, *James Connolly and the Reconquest of Ireland*.
8. J. Riddell, *Lenin's Struggle for a Revolutionary International* (New York: Monad, 1984), p. 378.
9. Padraig Yates, *Lockout Dublin 1913* (Dublin: Gill & Macmillian, 2000), p. 11.
10. Cronin, *Young Connolly*, p. 66.
11. Harry Diamond, *What Does the Irish Socialist Republican Party Stand For?* (Belfast: ISRP, no date).
12. Allen, *The Politics of James Connolly*, pp. 161–9. Anderson, *James Connolly and the Irish Left*, pp. 123–36.
13. Allen, *The Politics of James Connolly*, p. 178.
14. John Haney, *Charles Stewart Parnell* (New York: Chelsea House Publishers, 1989), p. 100.

The ISRP's Programme, 1896

'The great appear great to us only because we are on our knees;
LET US RISE.'

OBJECT

Establishment of AN IRISH SOCIALIST REPUBLIC based upon the public ownership by the Irish people of the land, and instruments of production, distribution and exchange. Agriculture to be administered as a public function, under boards of management elected by the agricultural population and responsible to them and to the nation at large. All other forms of labour necessary to the well-being of the community to be conducted on the same principles.

PROGRAMME

As a means of organising the forces of the Democracy in preparation for any struggle which may precede the realisation of our ideal, of paving the way for its realisation, of restricting the tide of emigration by providing employment at home, and finally of palliating the evils of our present social system, we work by political means to secure the following measures:

1. Nationalisation of railways and canals.

2. Abolition of private banks and money-lending institutions and establishment of state banks, under popularly elected boards of directors, issuing loans at cost.

3. Establishment at public expense of rural depots for the most improved agricultural machinery, to be lent out to the agricultural population at a rent covering cost and management alone.

4. Graduated income tax on all incomes over £400 per annum in order to provide funds for pensions to the aged, infirm and

widows and orphans.

5. Legislative restriction of hours of labour to 48 per week and establishment of a minimum wage.

6. Free maintenance for all children.

7. Gradual extension of the principle of public ownership and supply to all the necessaries of life.

8. Public control and management of National schools by boards elected by popular ballot for that purpose alone.

9. Free education up to the highest university grades.

10. Universal suffrage.

THE IRISH SOCIALIST REPUBLICAN PARTY

That the agricultural and industrial system of a free people, like their political system, ought to be an accurate reflex of the democratic principle by the people for the people, solely in the interests of the people.

That the private ownership, by a class, of the land and instruments of production, distribution and exchange, is opposed to this vital principle of justice, and is the fundamental basis of all oppression, national, political and social.

That the subjection of one nation to another, as of Ireland to the authority of the British Crown, is a barrier to the free political and economic development of the subjected nation, and can only serve the interests of the exploiting classes of both nations.

That, therefore, the national and economic freedom of the Irish people must be sought in the same direction, viz., the establishment of an Irish Socialist Republic, and the consequent conversion of the means of production, distribution and exchange into the common property of society, to be held and controlled by a democratic state in the interests of the entire community.

That the conquest by the Social Democracy of political power in Parliament, and on all public bodies in Ireland, is the readiest and most effective means whereby the revolutionary forces may be organised and disciplined to attain that end.

BRANCHES WANTED EVERYWHERE. ENQUIRIES INVITED. ENTRANCE FEE, 6d. MINIMUM. WEEKLY SUBSCRIPTION 1d. Offices: 67 MIDDLE ABBEY STREET, DUBLIN.

James Connolly's Wood Quay Election Address, January 1903

To The Electors

Fellow Workers,

Having been again asked to contest the Wood Quay Ward in the interests of labour, I desire, in accepting this invitation, to lay before you a few of the principles upon which I conducted the campaign last election, and on which I shall fight this.

Our defeat of last year, brought about as it was by a campaign of slander and bribery, and a wholesale and systematic debauching of the more degraded portion of the electorate, did not in the slightest degree affect the truth of the principles for which we contested. These principles still remain the only principles by which the working class can ever attain its freedom.

When the workers come into the world we find that we are outcasts in the world. The land on which we must live is the property of a class who are the descendants of men who stole the land from our forefathers, and we who are workers, are, whether in town or country, compelled to pay for permission to live on the earth; the houses, shops, factories, etc., which were built by the labour of our fathers at wages that simply kept them alive are now owned by a class which never contributed an ounce of sweat to their erecting, but whose members will continue to draw rent and profit from them while the system lasts. As a result of this the worker in order to live must sell himself into the service of a master – he must sell to that master the liberty to coin into profit the physical and mental energies.

A shopkeeper in order to live must sell his goods for what he can get, but a worker in order to live must sell a part of his life, nine, ten, or twelve hours per day as the case may be. The shopkeeper, if he is lucky, may get the value of his goods, but the worker cannot get under the capitalist system the value of his labour; he must accept whatever wage those who are unemployed are willing to accept at his job. This is what I call wage-slavery, because under it the worker is a slave who sells himself for a wage with which to buy his rations, which is the only difference between this system and negro slavery where the master bought the rations and fed the slave himself. There is only one remedy for this slavery of the working class, and that remedy is the socialist republic, a system of society in which the land and all houses, railways, factories, canals, workshops, and everything necessary for work shall be owned and operated as common property, much as the land of Ireland was owned by the clans of Ireland before England introduced the capitalist system amongst us at the point of the sword. There is only one way to attain that end, and that way is for the working class to establish a political party of its own; a political party which shall set itself to elect to all public bodies in Ireland working men resolved to use all the power of those bodies for the workers and against their oppressors, whether those oppressors be English, Scotch or sham Irish patriots. In claiming this we will only be following the example of our masters. Every political party is the party of a class. The Unionists represent the interests of the landlords and the big capitalists generally; the United Irish League is the party of the middle class, the agriculturists, the house jobbers, slum landlords, and drink sellers. If an Irish landlord evicts a tenant farmer he is denounced by the Home Rule press as an enemy to Ireland, but an Irish employer can lock out and attempt to starve thousands of true Irishmen, as was done in the building trade in 1896, in the tailoring trade in 1900, and in the engineers of Inchicore in 1902; and not a member of Parliament would take up the fight for the workers, or bother himself about them. Nay, the capitalists who thus try to crush their workers are highly honoured by the official parliamentary party, and some, like Mr. P. White, are members of the United Irish League Executive. If a man takes a farm from which a tenant has been evicted, he is rightly called a traitor, but who ever heard or read of the capitalist Home Rule press of this country saying a hard word about the scabs who go in on a strike or lock-out, even when those scabs were imported, as was the case during the tailors' lock-out, the saddlers' strike, or the engineers' lock-out? If the men who were imprisoned for threatening black-legs during the engineers' lock-out had been engaged in a dispute over farms, we would have been told that they were 'patriots suffering for their country'. But as they were only workmen fighting for their class interests, we were told by the Home Rule newspapers that they were 'misguided individuals'.

What is wanted then is for the workers to organise for political action on socialist lines. And let us take lesson by the municipal election of last year. Let us remember how the drinksellers of the Wood Quay Ward combined with the slum owner and the house jobber; let us remember how Alderman Davin, Councillor McCall, and all their fellow publicans issued free drinks to whoever would accept, until on the day before election and election day, the scenes of bestiality and drunkenness around their shops were such as brought the blush of shame to every decent man and woman who saw them. Let us remember the threats and the bribery, how Mr Byrne of Wood Quay told the surrounding tenants, that if 'Mr Connolly was elected their rents would be raised'; let us remember how the spirit of religion was prostituted to the service of the drinkseller to drive the labourer back into his degradation; how the workers were told that socialism and freethinking were the same thing, although the freethinking government of France was just after shooting down socialist workmen at Martinique for taking part in a strike procession; let us remember how the paid canvassers of the capitalist candidate – hired slanderers – gave a different account of Mr. Connolly to every section of the electors. How they said to the Catholics that he was an Orangeman, to the Protestants that he was a Fenian, to the Jews that he was an anti-Semite, to others that he was a Jew, to the labourers that he was a journalist on the make, and to the tradesmen and professional classes that he was an ignorant labourer; that he was born in Belfast, Derry, England, Scotland and Italy, according to the person the canvasser was talking to. Remember that all this carnival of corruption and dishonesty was resorted to, simply in order to prevent labour from electing a representative who could neither be bought, terrified nor seduced, and you will understand how important your masters conceive to be their hold on the public bodies in this country. You will also understand that there can never be either clean, healthy, or honest politics in the City of Dublin, until the power of the drinksellers is absolutely broken – they are positively the meanest and most degraded section that ever attempted to rule a city.

Now, Ladies and Gentlemen, you understand my position. This is socialist republicanism, the politics of labour, of freedom from all tyrants, foreign and native. If you are a worker your interests should compel you to vote for me, if you are a decent citizen, whether worker or master, you should vote for me; if you are an enemy of freedom, a tyrant, or the tool of a tyrant, you will vote against me.

Believing that in this fight I am fighting the fight of my class, I invite every self-respecting worker to join our committee and help the cause.

Yours in the name of labour,

JAMES CONNOLLY.

Bibliography

PRIMARY SOURCES

Dan O'Brien, *Public Health and Capitalism: Being the Report of a Lecture Delivered Before the Dublin Branch of the Irish Socialist Republican Party* (Dublin: *Workers Republic* Pamphlet, no date) LOP70 NLI

'The Early Propagandists of the ISRP Party', MS 15704 (i), O'Brien Collection, National Library of Ireland (NLI)

Minutes of the Irish Socialist Republican Party 1896–97, MS 13593, O'Brien Collection

Minutes of the Irish Socialist Republican Party, 1898–1904, MS 16264–67, O'Brien Collection

Minutes of the Socialist Party of Ireland, 1904, O'Brien Collection

Socialist Labour Party Declaration of Principals (Dublin, SLP, 1904). (NLI) LO P109 (27).

ISRP Election Manifesto in Hebrew (Dublin, ISRP, 1902) (NLI) ILB 300p11 (Item 80–81)

Irish Socialist Labour Party, William O'Brien (MS) NLI 15,674, 6 folders.

Newspapers

Shan Van Vocht, 1886–89
United Irishman, 1899–1906
Workers' Republic, 1898–1903

Connolly's Writings

Most of Connolly's writings appeared as articles and short pieces in various newspapers. Some have appeared as pamphlets and in collections.

Erin's Hope (New York: 1909) (publisher unknown)

Socialism and Nationalism (Dublin: Three Candlers, 1948)

Labour in Irish History (London: Bookmarks, 1987)

Socialism Made Easy (Dublin: The Plough Book Service, 1971)

Collected Works, two vols (Dublin: New Books Publications, 1987)

Proinsias Mac Aonghusa and Liam O'Reagain (eds), *The Best of Connolly* (Cork: Mercier Press, 1967)

Owen Dudley Edwards and Bernard Ransom (eds), *James Connolly: Selected Political Writings* (London: Cape, 1973)

Peter Berresford Ellis (ed.), *James Connolly: Selected Writings* (Harmondsworth: Penguin Books, 1973)

Websites

There are a number of websites that contain very good selections of Connolly's writings including:

http://www.marxists.org/archive/connolly/index.htm

www.wageslave.org/jcs

http://www.ucc.ie/celt/publishd.html#connolly

Secondary Sources

Kieran Allen, *The Politics of James Connolly* (London: Pluto Press, 1990)

Kieran Allen, *Is Ireland a Neo Colony?* (Dublin: Bookmarks, 1990)

Louis Althusser, *For Marx* (London: Norton, 1996)

Benedict Anderson, *Imagined Communities: Reflections on the Origin and Spread of Nationalism* (London: Verso, 1991)

W.K. Anderson, *James Connolly and the Irish Left* (Dublin: Irish Academic Press, 1994)

Chris Bambery, *Ireland's Permanent Revolution* (London: Bookmarks, 1990)

Peter Berresford Ellis, *A History of the Irish Working Class* (London: Pluto Press, 1996)

Liam Cahill, *Forgotten Revolution: The Limerick Soviet 1919* (Cork: O'Brien Press, 1991)

Helen Clarke, *Sing a Rebel Song: The Story of James Connolly* (Edinburgh: City of Edinburgh District Council and Irish History Workshop, 1989)

Tony Cliff, *Lenin: Building the Party (1893–1914)* (London: Bookmarks, 1994)

Tony Cliff, *Lenin 1917–23: Revolution Besieged* (London: Bookmarks, 1987)

Tony Cliff, *Rosa Luxemburg* (London: Bookmarks, 1986)

Sean Cronin, *Young Connolly* (Dublin: Repsol, 1983)

Mary Daly, *Dublin the Deposed Capital: A Social and Economic History 1860–1914* (Cork: Cork University Press, 1984)

Harry Diamond, *What Does the Irish Socialist Republican Party Stand For?* (Belfast: ISRP, no date)

Shaun Doherty, 'Will the Real James Connolly Please Stand Up', *International Socialism Journal* 80, Sept. 1998

P. Dubois, *Contemporary Ireland* (Dublin: Maunsell, 1908)

Owen Dudley Edwards, *James Connolly: The Mind of an Activist* (Dublin: Gill & Macmillan, 1971)

Richard Michael Fox, *James Connolly: The Forerunner* (Tralee: Kingdom Press, 1966)

C. Desmond Greaves, *The Life and Times of Connolly* (London: Lawrence & Wishart, 1971)

John Haney, *Charles Stewart Parnell* (New York: Chelsea House Publishers, 1989)

David Howell, *A Lost Left: Three Studies in Socialism and Nationalism* (Manchester: Manchester University Press, 1986)

Andy Johnston, James Larraghy and Edward McWilliams, *Connolly: A Marxist Analysis* (Dublin: Irish Workers Group, 1990)

Thomas Johnson, *Irish Labour and its International Relations in the Era of the Second International and the Bolshevik Revolution* (Cork: Cork Workers' Club, 1975)

James Joll, *The Second International* (London: Weidenfield & Nicolson, 1955)

Christine Kinealy, *This Great Calamity: The Irish Famine 1845–52* (Dublin: Gill & Macmillan, 1994)

Conor Kostick, *Popular Militancy in Ireland, 1917–23* (London: Pluto Press, 1997)

Fintan Lane, *The Origins of Modern Irish Socialism 1881–1896* (Cork: Cork University Press, 1997)

Joseph Lee, *The Modernisation of Irish Society (1848–1918)* (Dublin: Gill & Macmillan, 1973)

V.I. Lenin, *What is to be Done?* (Moscow: Progress Publishers, 1983)

V.I. Lenin, *Imperialism, the Highest Stage of Capitalism* (Moscow, Progress Publishers, 1983)

John Leslie, *The Present Position of the Irish Question* (Cork: Cork Workers Club, 1986)

Samuel Levenson, *James Connolly, Socialist, Patriot and Martyr* (London: Quartet, 1977)

F.S.L. Lyons, *Ireland Since the Famine* (London: Fontana Press, 1985).

George Lyons, *Some Recollections of Griffith and his Times* (Dublin: Talbot Press, 1923)

Proinsias Mac Aonghusa, *What Connolly Said* (Dublin: New Island Books, 1995)

Ernest Mandel, *Introduction to Marxism* (London: Ink Links, 1979)

Karl Marx and Frederick Engels, *Ireland and the Irish Question* (Moscow: Progress Publishers, 1971)

Donal McCartney (ed.), *Parnell: The Politics of Power* (Dublin: Wolfhound Press, 1991)

Priscilla Metscher, *James Connolly and the Reconquest of Ireland* (Minnesota: Marxist Educational Press/Nature, Society and Thought, 2002)

Austen Morgan, *Political Biography of James Connolly* (Manchester: Manchester University Press, 1988)

John Muldoon and George McSweeney, *A Guide to the Elections of County and Rural District Councillors in Ireland* (Dublin: Easons & Son, 1902)

K.B. Nowlan, *The Making of 1916: Studies in the History of the Rising* (Dublin: Stationery Office, 1969)

William O'Brien, *Forth the Banners Go* (Dublin: Three Candles, 1969)

Sean O' Casey, *Autobiographies 1* (New York: Carroll & Graf, 1984)

Emmett O'Connor, *A Labour History of Ireland 1824–1960* (Cork: Cork University Press, 1992)

Thomas Pakenham, *The Boer War* (New York: Random House, 1979)

Belinda Probert, *Beyond Orange and Green* (London: Academy Press, 1978)

John Rees, *The Algebra of Revolution The Dialectic and the Classical Marxist Tradition* (London: Routledge, 1998)

J. Riddell, *Lenin's Struggle for a Revolutionary International* (New York: Monad, 1984)

Laurence H. Simon (ed.), *Karl Marx: Selected Writings* (Cambridge: Hackett Publishing Company, 1994)

Leon Trotsky, *The History of the Russian Revolution* (London: Pluto Press, 1977)

Mary-Alice Waters (ed.), *Rosa Luxemburg Speaks* (New York: Pathfinder Press, 1970)

Padraig Yates, *Lockout Dublin 1913* (Dublin: Gill & Macmillan, 2000)

Index